ART AND SPIRITUALITY

CAC Publishing
Center for Action and Contemplation
cac.org

"*Oneing*" is an old English word that was used by Lady Julian of Norwich (1342–1416) to describe the encounter between God and the soul. The Center for Action and Contemplation proudly borrows the word to express the divine unity that stands behind all of the divisions, dichotomies, and dualisms in the world. We pray and publish with Jesus' words, "that all may be one" (John 17:21).

On the cover:
Arroyo Hondo Reredo, Marie Romero Cash, 1985, 27 x 25 in., Santa Maria de la Vid Abbey, NM. Used with permission.

EDITOR:
Vanessa Guerin

ASSOCIATE EDITOR:
Shirin McArthur

PUBLISHER:
The Center for Action and Contemplation

ADVISORY BOARD:
David Benner
James Danaher
Ilia Delio, OSF
Sheryl Fullerton
Stephen Gaertner, OPraem
Ruth Patterson

Design and Composition by Nelson Kane

© 2024 Center for Action and Contemplation.
All rights reserved.

Oneing
An Alternative Orthodoxy

The biannual literary journal of the Center for Action and Contemplation.

The Perennial Tradition, Vol. 1, No. 1, Spring 2013

Ripening, Vol. 1, No. 2, Fall 2013

Transgression, Vol. 2, No. 1, Spring 2014

Evidence, Vol. 2, No. 2, Fall 2014

Emancipation, Vol. 3, No. 1, Spring 2015

Innocence, Vol. 3, No. 2, Fall 2015

Perfection, Vol. 4, No. 1, Spring 2016

Evolutionary Thinking, Vol. 4, No. 2, Fall 2016

Transformation, Vol. 5, No. 1, Spring 2017

Politics and Religion, Vol. 5, No. 2, Fall 2017

Anger, Vol. 6, No. 1, Spring 2018

Unity and Diversity, Vol. 6, No. 2, Fall 2018

The Universal Christ, Vol. 7, No. 1, Spring 2019

The Future of Christianity, Vol. 7, No. 2, Fall 2019

Liminal Space, Vol. 8, No. 1, Spring 2020

Order, Disorder, Reorder, Vol. 8, No. 2, Fall 2020

Trauma, Vol. 9, No. 1, Spring 2021

The Cosmic Egg, Vol. 9, No. 2, Fall 2021

Unveiled, Vol. 10, No. 1, Spring 2022

Nonviolence, Vol. 10, No. 2, Fall 2022

Transitions, Vol. 11, No. 1, Spring 2023

Falling Upward, Vol. 11, No. 2, Fall 2023

Oneing is a limited-issue publication; therefore, some issues are no longer in print. To order available issues of *Oneing*, please visit https://store.cac.org/collections/oneing.

Oneing

VOLUME 12 NO. 1

SHIRIN MCARTHUR
    Introduction: An Interview with Paul Swanson
    and Brandon Strange   17

TEDDY MACKER
    Accordion   25

LOURDES BERNARD
    Artmaking as Contemplative Praxis   27

RICHARD ROHR
    The Artist's Access to Mystery   35

FELICIA MURRELL
    The Art of Food   39

JOSH RADNOR
    Joshua: 45-46   47

MARIE ROMERO CASH
    Discovering My Soul   51

CATHERINE DOWLING
    With New Eyes   57

SCOTT AVETT
    Creating Faithfully   71

JENNA KEIPER
    When Body Speaks:
    On Dance as Spiritual Practice   77

MARK LONGHURST
   Meeting a Creative God in the Arts   87

JOEL GARNER
   The Abbey as Art Repository   93

KARLA CAVARRA BRITTON
   The Persistent Resurgence of Sacred Architecture   101

STEPHEN PAVEY
   Visual Storytelling and Walking with the Oppressed:
   A Journey to Our Sacred Unity   111

DREW JACKSON
   As I Sit Thinking in the Car   117

RECOMMENDED READING
   Art + Faith: A Theology of Making
   A Book Review by Lee Staman   119

RECOMMENDED VIEWING
   American Symphony
   A Film Review by Paul Swanson   123

NOTES   127

ACKNOWLEDGMENTS   133

EDITOR'S NOTE

It's hard to believe that over ten years have passed since CAC Publishing introduced *Oneing* to its US and international audience—a publication initially designed to showcase the amazing authors first published in *Radical Grace*, a newsletter conceived by Fr. Richard Rohr over thirty-six years ago.

It was Fr. Richard who suggested the title *Oneing* for this literary journal, a word used by his favorite mystic, Lady Julian of Norwich (1342–1416), to describe the encounter between God and the soul. In addition to serving as cocurator for the publication, he wrote the Introduction for each issue and contributed an occasional article. In 2022, as his health was failing and he began stepping back from active participation in the work of the CAC, he relinquished this role. The first guest cocurator, Fr. John Dear, was invited to contribute the Introduction and suggest authors for the Fall issue on Nonviolence. Invited guest cocurators have continued to take this role for each subsequent issue.

For this Spring 2024 issue of *Oneing* on Art and Spirituality, gifted staff members Brandon Strange and Paul Swanson cocurated it with me and were interviewed for the Introduction by Associate Editor Shirin McArthur. Additionally, they recommended many of the impressive authors and artists featured in this exceptional issue of the journal—the first to feature images of art and architecture.

Inspired by my own background in and love for art and spirituality, I decided that this, my final issue as Editor of *Oneing*, would highlight this theme and become my swan song as I transitioned away from the CAC in January 2024 after twenty years of service to this fine organization.

O NE OF THE artists suggested by Brandon Strange was Lourdes Bernard—a well-established Dominican American artist. As it turned out, I had already developed an interest in her fascinating work before I discovered she'd attended CAC's Living School. Trained as an architect, her drawings are at once conceptually complex, satirical, and historically and politically relevant. In her article "Artmaking as Contemplative Praxis," Bernard writes:

> Art invites audiences to consider the spirituality and transformative power of images. Engaging art offers respite, contemplation, even as it shares powerful, inspiring, or difficult stories. Art images are real and alive and have the power to change us and cause change . . . [and] they can shift our perspective on what we thought we knew and understood about a subject. Too often, art is considered decorative, and it is significantly more than that. Engaging with art means we have to slow down to allow a new experience to enter which perhaps cannot be accessed in another way. It can be an expansive experience.

Another multi-talented artist whose work may be familiar to our readership is Scott Avett of The Avett Brothers fame. Like Bernard, his impressive paintings emanate from lived experiences. In his beautifully written article "Creating Faithfully," Avett writes:

> Painting is like living. . . . An idea is born, an invitation accepted, and a devotion sustained in a mysterious gift of joy and suffering, from its inception to its end. It is in the deepest and darkest moments of this mystery that I may feel the heaviest of doubts, but I long to create faithfully. To create faithfully, I am asked to follow an idea into darkness, not knowing where it will go or what may come of me. To enter into this mysterious exchange is faith itself.

Growing up in Latin America, I became interested in architecture at a very early age. By the time I was eight years old, I had committed to memory the expansive boulevards and massive buildings in Santiago, Chile. So, as I considered contributors for this issue, I was inspired to invite architectural historian Karla Britton to submit a piece on Rafael Moneo's magnificent minimalist Iesu Church in San Sebastian, Spain. Although she writes about Moneo, she also addresses the work of other important architects and their major projects in her article "The Persistent Resurgence of Sacred Architecture." Britton's article inspired this reader to want to visit and revisit many magnificent architectural structures, particularly Moneo's Cathedral of Our Lady of the Angels in Los Angeles and John Gaw Meem's Pueblo Revival Style buildings here in New Mexico—representations of which can be seen at the University of New Mexico (Zimmerman Library) and Los Poblanos Historic Inn.

These are only a few examples of the many exciting contributions to this issue of *Oneing*, which also includes moving poetic prose by CAC staff member Jenna Keiper and the timely and powerful poetry of Teddy Macker, a notable recommendation by Paul Swanson, who, in addition to his interview and contributor recommendations, reviewed the amazing documentary film "American Symphony."

I am deeply grateful to both Paul Swanson and Brandon Strange for collaborating with me on this, my final production of *Oneing*. I hope you will enjoy each contribution as if it were a hologram of a work of art.

Vanessa Guerin
Editor, *Oneing*

CONTRIBUTORS

BRANDON STRANGE has served as the Director of Engagement at the Center for Action and Contemplation since 2019. He has also worked as a freelance web designer and as Marketing Manager for the Long Center for the Performing Arts in Austin, Texas. Born and raised in Oklahoma, Brandon now lives in Albuquerque, New Mexico, with his wife Erin.

PAUL SWANSON is Lead Program Designer at the Center for Action and Contemplation. He is a jackleg Mennonite and a part of the Community of the Incarnation. Paul and his wife Laura have two feral, but beloved, children who know a thing or two about contemplation as the immediacy of life. Learn more about his work kindling the examined life for contemplatives in the world at http://www.contemplify.com.

SHIRIN MCARTHUR is an Episcopal editor, writer coach, spiritual guide, and retreat leader who lives in Arizona and ponders the sacred through poetry, photography, nature, and contemplation. She holds a Master of Divinity degree from Boston University School of Theology and a Certificate in Spiritual Guidance from the Shalem Institute. Shirin serves on the core faculty team of the Hesychia School for Spiritual Direction. She is also a former CAC staff member and the Associate Editor of *Oneing*. To learn more about Shirin McArthur, visit https://shirinmcarthur.com/.

TEDDY MACKER is the author of the collection of poetry *This World*. His other writings appear widely in the *Los Angeles Times*, *Orion*, *The Sun*, *Tin House*, and elsewhere. For many years, Teddy taught literature at the University of California Santa Barbara. He lives with his wife and daughters on a small farm in Carpinteria, California, where he maintains an orchard. His second collection of poetry, *Only Mystery*, is forthcoming through Archimboldi. To learn more about Teddy Macker, visit https://www.massreview.org/node/9852.

LOURDES BERNARD is a Dominican American artist whose multimedia works address how historical events take shape within a landscape. Her research-based practice unravels complex histories through visual storytelling. A graduate of Syracuse University School of Architecture and the New York Studio School, Lourdes has exhibited in numerous New York venues and received the following awards: Yaddo Foundation Fellowship, Wurlitzer Foundation Fellowship, 2023 National Association of Latino Arts and Cultures Fund for the Arts, and 2024 New York State Council on the Arts. Lourdes' project "The Women of April" exhibited in the New York Studio School gallery, then traveled to the Erdman Center at Princeton Theological Seminary, where she is currently artist in residence. To learn more about Lourdes Bernard, visit https://www.lourdesbernard.com/.

RICHARD ROHR, OFM is a Franciscan priest and the Founder of the Center for Action and Contemplation in Albuquerque, New Mexico. An internationally recognized author and spiritual leader, Fr. Richard teaches primarily on incarnational mysticism, nondual consciousness, and contemplation, with a particular emphasis on how these affect the social justice issues of our time. Along with many recorded conferences, he is the author of numerous books, including *The Universal Christ: How a Forgotten Reality Can Change Everything We See, Hope For, and Believe* and *The Wisdom Pattern: Order, Disorder, Reorder*. To learn more about Fr. Richard Rohr and the CAC, visit https://cac.org/richard-rohr/richard-rohr-ofm/.

FELICIA MURRELL, a 2022 sendee of the Center for Action and Contemplation's Living School, is a certified master life coach and spiritual companion. As a former ordained pastor, she has over twenty years of church leadership experience and now serves the global community with a message of inclusion and integration. Felicia is a freelance copy editor and the author of *Truth Encounters* and her newest book, *And: The Restorative Power of Love in an Either/Or World*. She and her husband Doug reside in the Twin Cities, Minnesota. They are the parents of four adult children. To read more from Felicia Murrell, visit https://www.instagram.com/hellofelicia_murrell/.

JOSH RADNOR is an actor, writer, director, and musician. As an actor, he has starred in long-running television shows (*How I Met Your Mother*), short-running television shows (*Hunters, Rise, Mercy Street*), films (Joey Soloway's *Afternoon Delight*), on Broadway (*The Graduate, Disgraced*) and off Broadway. He wrote and directed two feature films (*happythankyoumoreplease* and *Liberal Arts*), both of which premiered at the Sundance Film Festival, the former winning the 2010 Audience Award. Josh made two albums with Australian musician Ben Lee as Radnor & Lee. His solo EP "One More

Then I'll Let You Go" was released in 2021. *Eulogy: Volume 1*, his debut solo LP, was released in 2023. To learn more about Josh Radnor, visit https://en.wikipedia.org/wiki/Josh_Radnor.

MARIE ROMERO CASH is one of New Mexico's most renowned *santeras*, award-winning folk artists, and authors, whose colorful works are in major museums and private collections. Her work can be seen at the Museum of Spanish Colonial Art, the Museum of International Folk Art, the Peyton Wright Gallery, the Smithsonian in Washington, DC, and the Vatican. Marie has participated in the annual Traditional Spanish Market in Santa Fe, New Mexico for over forty-five years, where she has won many awards for both traditional and contemporary works. She has written numerous books and articles on the culture and religious art of Northern New Mexico and has also authored a series of mysteries. To learn more about Marie Romero Cash, visit https://marieromerocash.com/.

CATHERINE DOWLING was born in Ireland and has divided her life between the United States and her home country. She has a Master of Arts in history from the University of Montana and subsequently worked hard to create a checkered resume that includes writing, waitressing, quality assurance, teaching, and psychotherapy. Catherine has published two books: *Radical Awareness: Five Practices for a Fully Engaged Life* and *Rebirthing and Breathwork: A Powerful Technique for Personal Transformation*. Her articles have appeared in *Oneing, Rkvry, Positive Health, Inside Out, Lowestoft Chronicle, Montana Mouthful, HerStry*, and more. She resides in Ireland. To learn more about Catherine Dowling, visit http://www.catherinedowling.com/.

SCOTT AVETT was born in Cheyenne, Wyoming, and raised in rural North Carolina. His father worked as a welder and his mother as a reading teacher. They cultivated a home that nurtured artistic pursuit. Scott is well known as a founding member of The Avett Brothers, but he is also an accomplished visual artist. He attended East Carolina University, where he studied journalistic broadcasting and painting. After Scott received a communications degree in 1999, painter Leland Wallin convinced him to pursue a career in visual art, and Scott has been painting and printmaking ever since. His work is largely figurative, with a focus on spirituality and familial and interpersonal relationships. Scott resides in North Carolina with his wife and three children. To learn more about Scott Avett, visit https://www.scottavett.com/.

JENNA KEIPER, Multimedia Producer at the CAC, is an interdisciplinary artist and director who creates from the intersection of live performance, digital media, and visual anthropology. Raised in the Pacific Northwest, educated in Los Angeles, and expanded in Germany and Albuquerque, New Mexico, she follows the threads of spirituality, psychology, kinesiology, and somatic expression to create multimedia that explores the poetry of being. Whether through dance performance (Bachelor of Fine Arts) or visual anthropology and film (Master of Arts), Jenna finds her way to the space in between art and social science. To learn more about Jenna Keiper, visit https://www.jennakeiper.com/.

MARK LONGHURST is the Print and Digital Publications Manager at the CAC and the author of the forthcoming book *The Holy Ordinary: A Way to God* (Monkfish Publishing, October 2024). Before coming to the CAC, Mark spent a decade working for social justice nonprofits in Boston and a decade pastoring United Church of Christ churches in Western Massachusetts. An avid reader, he is a husband and dad, a yoga enthusiast, and a lover of contemporary art. You can follow Mark's writing at marklonghurst.substack.com and on Instagram at ordinary.mystic.

ABBOT JOEL GARNER, OPraem is the first abbot of Santa Maria de la Vid Abbey and the last of the five founding members of the Norbertine Community of New Mexico. He holds a doctorate in Religion and Education from Columbia University and Union Theological Seminary in New York City as well as a Master of Arts in Theology from Marquette University. Abbot Joel has served as a college teacher, campus minister, seminary formation director, and pastor over the years. To learn more about Abbot Joel Garner and the Norbertine Abbey, visit www.norbertinecommunity.org.

KARLA CAVARRA BRITTON is Professor of Art History at Diné College on the Navajo Nation and Dean of its School of Arts and Humanities. With a PhD in architectural history from Harvard University, she first directed Columbia University's architecture program in Paris before joining the faculty of the Yale School of Architecture. There, Karla developed a focus on contemporary sacred architecture, convening an interdisciplinary symposium that resulted in the book *Constructing the Ineffable*. She has published numerous articles on religious architecture, including works by Auguste Perret, Le Corbusier, Paul Rudolph, and John Gaw Meem. Karla lives in Tsaile, Arizona and Albuquerque, New Mexico. To learn more about Karla Cavarra Britton, visit https://lib.dinecollege.edu/blog/Faculty-Research-Highlights-Dr-Karla-Britton.

STEPHEN PAVEY, MDiv, PhD, is a photographer, a witness, an artist, and a mystic—all of which come together in the vocation of cultivating a way to see in order to bear witness to the world both as it is and as it could be. His visual storytelling focuses on hope—hope found in the struggle and dignity of becoming more human. Stephen loves to hike and canoe in the wilderness, ferment vegetables, play board games, and build things with his hands. To learn more about Stephen Pavey, visit https://www.stevepavey.com/index.

DREW E. JACKSON is a poet, speaker, and public theologian. He is author of *God Speaks Through Wombs: Poems on God's Unexpected Coming* and *Touch the Earth: Poems on The Way*. Drew's work has appeared in *Oneing, The Isolation Journals with Suleika Jaouad, Made for Pax, The Journal from the Centre for Public Christianity, Fathom Magazine,* and other publications. He received his Bachelor of Arts in Political Science from the University of Chicago and his Master of Arts in Theology from Fuller Theological Seminary. Drew currently works as the Director of Mission Integration for the Center for Action and Contemplation and lives in Brooklyn, New York with his wife and daughters. To learn more about Drew E. Jackson, visit https://drewejackson.com/.

LEE STAMAN is the Library Director at the Center for Action and Contemplation. He focuses on cataloging, preserving, and making accessible all Richard Rohr's work. Lee earned degrees in philosophy and theology before studying library science at the University of Washington. While there, his in-depth study of a nineteenth-century Torah from the Arabian Peninsula ignited a passion for the further study of Judaism along with the beliefs and practices of smaller religious communities. Lee's interests include Wendell Berry, the Premier League, biblical studies, and books about books. He resides in Seattle, Washington with his wife and children. Lee Staman may be contacted at lstaman@cac.org.

INTRODUCTION

CAC staff members Brandon Strange and Paul Swanson are interviewed by Oneing Associate Editor Shirin McArthur on their perspectives on art and spirituality.

Brandon Strange: I have a strong skeptical—but not cynical—perspective on art. I love story. For the longest time, through fiction and writing, I found magic in the connection between meaning and the visual representation of that meaning through words and letters. I wanted to zoom in and see how it actually works, because there's so much more that happens with the transmission of meaning when you have words on a page. So, I loved large, complex novels that would explore and even interrogate the format and the medium themselves.

Eventually, I ended up at a place where I saw every writer and novel as phony—and I connect that with capitalism, which makes art really challenging. It's very difficult to be an artist these days. It's so much easier to be someone who is into aesthetics and curating sensory experiences or stylizing products.

This meant I tended to start at a skeptical place when I was assessing a new art form, especially poetry. I have personally run around with too many people for whom it wasn't about the work itself, but about the idea they had of themselves as a poet. Then I had to recognize that I too was infatuated with the idea of being an author, with the ability to provide for myself, to have that influence.

I sense it would be challenging to create something new in a time when there aren't a lot of rules around what art is and should be. This relates to how capitalism commodifies things. When you're trying to capture the ineffable and communicate something that can't actually be spoken or communicated—only *spoken around*, so to speak—you run up against the imperative of turning things into commodities that are meant to appeal to people, that are meant to be sold. We hear, "Keep your audience in mind. What's the market for these sorts of things?"

This is coupled with the fact that we live in a society where people are not used to being challenged through what they consume. The Internet has opened so many doors and broken down barriers. I don't have to get signed to a publishing house to be an author. I can do it myself. But it's also knocked down a lot of the structures and scaffolding that formed a shared set of assumptions about what something is going to be and whether they expect to be challenged by it. Most people are looking for satisfaction by getting that serotonin rush—a much more widespread consumer orientation.

That's challenging to navigate as an artist. I think you have to both cater to and undermine it, which requires an awareness of the thing itself that you're undermining. Plus, the Internet is still so new. It is a consciousness that's still developing on a cultural level.

Shirin McArthur: Please say more about what you mean by rules.

Brandon: A good example is the idea of genre. In literature, genre is a set of rules, so to speak. There are certain expectations that come into play around engaging with the work of a particular genre of fiction. What are readers' expectations? Why are they coming to that genre? What are they hoping to experience? Writers play inside the structure created by these expectations. A common online quote is that you have to learn the rules of something before you can undermine or subvert them. That's because the purpose isn't to just break these rules, but to bend or break them in ways that create levels of meaning.

Paul Swanson: So, you're saying that the absence of genre or a way to categorize art can lead to such a fragmentation that anything can be considered art? There's the dissolution of art when everything is art, in that kind of postmodern, meta-modern way?

Brandon: Yes. If everything is art, is anything art?

Shirin: Paul, would you share your thoughts on this theme as it connects with your Contemplify podcast[1]? Have any of your interviews connected with art in ways that have been impactful?

Paul: I love talking to artists because I feel like artists and contemplatives are stitched together in very natural ways. It's often easier to talk to an artist than a theologian because a theologian knows that they're supposed to be a theologian, so they'll try to give concrete answers, whereas artists and contemplatives will give responses that leave room for mystery and the unknown. I think a good theologian will do that as well, but sometimes theologians will try to make sure every peg fits.

I love talking to artists who carry that contemplative spirit in that they see their practice or medium—whether it's music or poetry or literature—as their contemplative practice. It helps them shed the falsities that get in the way of their interior self or their soul or their connection to God. There are opportunities for grace and freedom.

I love talking to poets. Getting back to capitalism and art, one thing about poets is that they never make money—unless they are Mary Oliver. Yet it requires giving so much of yourself over to your art. Jim Harrison (1937–2016) would talk about that to younger poets who'd ask for advice. He would say, "Are you willing to give all your life over to this craft?" I think that's very similar to a contemplative: Are you willing to surrender all to deepen the mystery? That's a very daunting ask.

I am most interested in poetry that quakes me and takes my breath away, where there's a physical reaction. My favorite poet the past few years has been Teddy Macker [whose work is included in this issue of *Oneing*]. He is also a teacher and an orchardist. Macker writes so incarnationally about the human experience and that connection to the divine in *this world*. His first book of poetry is titled *This World*, and it's so deeply religious without being dogmatic. When he uses religious terms, they expand into sensory explosions of feeling and passion while also acknowledging the apophatic: the mystery that words aren't enough, in the void and vastness and nothingness.

I think it's very hard to contain that in a poem. It's the ambience you're left with after a poem, where you feel it in the air and can taste it. That is why I seek out poetry and poets, because they're trying to be so present to the reality in front of them and be clear-eyed and open-eyed to it.

Richard Rohr talks about the personal as the gateway to the universal, and I think that is part of the necessity of poets. I would love to see poets get more due respect in our times.

Brandon: Paul, what are the sorts of things that a poem does to give you those feelings or strike you as incarnational? Is it something that changes, and you have to sense it, or is there a pattern to it?

Paul: Thomas Merton (1915–1968) told this story about when a Sufi master came to visit the monastery and met the novices. When the Sufi master left, Merton said, "We don't make them like that anymore," as in, "He has the sense of a desert father." I love that visceral image. A poem like that leaves a scent.

Right now, I'm reading this book of poetry by Donald Hall (1928–2018) called *Without*. He wrote it after his wife, Jane Kenyon (1947–1995), passed away. All the poems are about that journey toward *without* and the absence of presence. I have never had that experience, but I have had the experience of the presence of absence and the absence of presence. It slows down all urgency in my life for more of an immediacy. I am left with a change in how I view the room around me, my relationships, waiting in line, the slant of light. I think about the ways in which all of life starts to vibrate with God. I'm left with all the things that arise for me, and then I get to examine and feel and stretch out in different ways.

The poetry to which I am most drawn is written by those who spend a lot of time in nature. Not that they would necessarily consider themselves nature poets—they might—but those who are familiar enough and humble enough to realize that they're just a small part of this fabric of all creation and who can communicate that in a particular way with a particular voice.

Sometimes Jim Harrison was unpredictable. He'd express everything in one sentence, something to the point of, "A life lived rightly is a river." I note just what that imagery does, because I love water, I love rivers. And what does that line mean? If you live your life correctly, you are a river, with all the bends and all the stops and all the ways that things get into it. Sometimes they're poisoned, and sometimes we have to restore them. I sense that a good poem will take me to corners that I haven't examined.

Brandon: I have felt good art communicates something ineffable. Listening to you just now, I'm reconsidering that, in the sense that good art is something that raises our consciousness, that brings us to a greater awareness of something. In literature, I would say that it names something that perhaps previously went unnamed.

Some of the most impactful poetry for me were song lyrics, helped along by the music. There's something about the precision of naming. I recognized what they were speaking of, and then I got to name it in that same way.

Richard Rohr wrote,

> I believe that the combination of human action from a contemplative center is the greatest art form. It underlies all those other, more visible art forms that we see in great sculpture, music, writing, painting, and, most especially, in the art form called human character. When action and contemplation are united, we always have beauty, symmetry, and transformation—lives and actions that inherently sparkle and heal, even with dark images.[2]

Paul: Music has been one of the ways through which I've been able to express what I wasn't able to fully own or feel yet. I think about those times I thought, "That's why I'm drawn to this song: because it's speaking to what I can't put into words." It's fun now, as a father, to watch my daughter discover music that she likes on her own, not just the music that I forced upon her. She will ask for certain songs now, and I've made a very conscious choice to learn the lyrics of the songs that she loves so that I can sing along, even though they may not move me, or I may not understand. How can I join her in the participation, the seeking that happens in her own being drawn to certain art?

I love going to live music, with the experience of everyone gathering and what can happen with the hush of a crowd or when everyone's singing together or sharing the silence after a song. There's a reverence that I very much appreciate.

Brandon: There's the validation too, of going from the feeling of, "Oh, that's what I'm feeling," to "Oh, I'm not alone," to "There's a whole community of people who are feeling the same thing." I went to many shows for that connection to community and the way it validated and supported me through one period of my life.

Shirin: In terms of community, there's often a sense or assumption with many art forms that the artist is an individual when they're creating art. They have to have their process. Many hide themselves away or go into a "locked room." I'm curious what that raises for you in terms of the spiritual life and the sense of community.

Brandon: What comes to my mind immediately is that idea of going out and returning. One of the reasons why the hero's journey still resonates with so many people in so many different contexts and cultures is because there's something fundamental about that idea of going out and coming back. It can't be either individuals only or communal only. You have to go out and then bring back what you learned or where you came from.

When I think of the artist locking themselves away for six months to write something, there's almost something aesthetic to it, like a shedding, trying to seek out a pure, truer vision that requires going out so you can have that perspective and see those new things that you couldn't see when you were in the crowd.

Paul: Community can play an important role in creativity. I immediately thought about the band The Roots and how they rose to a certain level of notoriety, but there was no clear genre for their music. Their style of music was not easily found in what was popular at the time. So, they did something brilliant. They set up a residency in Philadelphia and created a scene. They brought in other artists who were kindred spirits and had high levels of musicianship, connection, and lyricism, and they created a scene there. Suddenly, this was a place for artists to launch out of.

I think the same thing can be said about Richard Rohr. He's a Franciscan. There are some people who see him as this singular teacher, but he was formed in this deep tradition. I also think about my own formation. The communities I've been a part of have helped me find my gifts. My growth came about in ways that couldn't have happened without those mirrors—and hopefully I've been the same for them.

There's a gift in artistic community, and there's a certain mythic quality to the idea that only lone artists are doing their thing. I think the same thing is true of the Western myth of contemplation, of shutting the world off and going to be alone, whether that be aspects of solitude or touching beyond time—whether it's the great cloud of witnesses or mystics of the past. Yet we are touching the entire world through the heart of prayer. Contemplation is not to escape the world, but to return with more vibrancy of life.

There's this line from Matsuo Bashō (1644–1694) that I love, "Stay in the world to transcend the world." Of course, I learned that from another poet, Chris Dombrowski. Those touchstones of conversations create this kaleidoscope to see the multi-vocality of contemplative artistic expression. You can get very excited about finding it everywhere, but we need that community so we don't get stuck in saying, "The contemplative path is this" or "The artistic path is this."

Life is constantly teaching you and inviting you into wider community and deeper expression. I do feel artists get there first. Contemplatives are in that loop too. They may not always be able to articulate it, but they hint at it. They can smell that scent or hear those whispers.

Brandon: I love that you used the word conversation because that's a key piece. Even at that most extreme end, when someone is leaving and isolating themselves, there's still the question of who they are creating art for. They're coming back. There's the audience. Are you an artist if you go out, think about all these things, and then never share them? No. That conversational piece is key for art. It's what really drew me to fiction—the idea that in finding shared meaning, we actually break down the barriers between us.

Paul: I've been taking my kids to the Albuquerque Museum. I think about these artists' lives and work speaking to my kids, who are eight and four. For some reason, they are absorbed by what is being communicated through the piece before them. It's a conversation that is present but started sometime 300 years ago or whenever that piece was created. I love the bendiness of how art can affect us. My kids may have a very vivid experience or response to it, and I may not. Suddenly, the conversation that started 300 years ago is creating a new conversation between us about what something means. Why were you so drawn to that? What does that make you want to do?

Then they go home, and maybe they create their own piece inspired by that conversation. Now they're carrying that piece with them as a part of their own human artistic conversation in the world. I get rather geeked out by that: the ripple effect or the body of Christ living out in that way in this world.

Brandon: That conversation between individuals and God, and individuals with each other, creates a web of shared meaning through time. Suddenly, anything in the world can become a medium for art because whatever we're using to communicate a piece of the ineffable suddenly becomes art.

So, what is an artist? I think an artist is a human being who moves through reality in that way. It almost seems too restrictive to call only artists "artists." I think it's more of a mode of how we are to engage with God and spirit in the natural world ourselves and how that gets communicated and stitched together with other people. •

Accordion

    There are no more roses anymore,
     even though there are roses.
     Fastly tightening, people looking down
     into their hands, styrofoam everywhere,
     energy drinks, plexiglass, porn,
     there are no more accordions,
     no more bluebirds, no more freckled girls
     under streetlights in spring.
     Even though there are freckled girls
     and rivers, rivers of water. But we—
    we must make prayers again.
     The navel of every human
     is lonely. The innocent countries
     of the back. Shoulders
     like night-quiet pines.
     Don't ask for God.
     Don't ask for happiness
     or liberation. When you pray,
     ask for the world
     to return to your eyes.

    —Teddy Macker[1]

The Annunciation with Four Marys and One Mario, Lourdes Bernard, 2023, 40 x 48 in., graphite on paper. Artist's collection. Used with permission.

Artmaking as Contemplative Praxis

By Lourdes Bernard

Art is singular. Art invites us to know beauty and to solicit it, summon it, from even the most tragic of circumstances. The best art is political and you ought to be able to make it unquestionably political and irrevocably beautiful at the same time.

—Toni Morrison

ART AND SPIRITUALITY

ART IS SINGULAR

The practice of Menju (face-to-face transmission) is a ceremony in Zen Buddhism where the *dharma* or truth is "transmitted" to the student by the teacher. In actuality, it is less about a transmission and more about a mystical seeing and a spiritual recognition during a face-to-face encounter. Historically, the encounters were recorded and became part of the spiritual lineage of passing along the *dharma* in Buddhist communities. The lineage stories are called *rokus*, which means records.

Aesthetic encounters are equally transformative, which is to say that a viewer can experience an emotional, spiritual, or psychological shift upon encountering a particular work of art. In this way, art can have a healing impact and elicit a powerful positive response. For me, works like Diego Velasquez' "Christ Crucified" at El Prado and the monumental works of Julie Mehretu and Maria Magdalena Campos-Pon offer me a transformative spiritual experience, time and again. After sitting with their art, I am moved and fundamentally different in a way that can only be triggered by viewing compelling art. Today, we are inundated with images, and yet it is through images that we process information that allows us to understand our world and, in turn, to make societal changes.

In this article, I want to discuss audience engagement and participation in art projects, artmaking as a spiritual and contemplative praxis in the studio, and how this dialogue between artist and audience is a catalyst for societal change. Art is deeply rooted in shared lived experiences as well as in the imagination. Art reveals culture, mirrors society's vulnerabilities, celebrates our humanity, and is truthful.

Similar to our experience of nature, art is the spiritual made tangible. Artmaking is a manifestation, a record of a spiritual conversation in the studio that simultaneously involves hand, eye, mind, body, and heart during the making and birthing of an image. Artmaking is spiritual praxis. It is this combination of energies that can potentially live in the image or the work, physically expressed as marks, color, form, materiality, and narrative content (when that is the focus of the work).

Artmaking is both physical labor and contemplative praxis. As an artist, I've discovered that the work is its own thing, and I strive to be faithful to the work. In that sense, there can be an intention but not an agenda or ego while making the work. The art stems from an authentic curiosity and an honest exploration, a discovery and a fresh response to a subject, an environment or idea. For me, having a formal contemplative practice makes this possible, although it doesn't make it easy. I think there is a faithfulness and a devotion in the practice of artmaking which can feel monastic while simultaneously linking us back to the world and to God.

ART'S INVITATION

ART INVITES AUDIENCES to consider the spirituality and transformative power of images. Engaging art offers respite, contemplation, even as it shares powerful, inspiring, or difficult stories. Art images are real and alive and have the power to change us and cause change. As I noted earlier, they can shift our perspective on what we thought we knew and understood about a subject. Too often, art is considered decorative, and it is significantly more than that. Engaging with art means we have to slow down to allow a new experience to enter which perhaps cannot be accessed in another way. It can be an expansive experience.

Sometimes the artwork is simply a place where particular issues, ideas, and problems can live. The work offers no solutions, as that's not what art is. This reminds me of the quote attributed to Pablo Picasso (1881–1973): "Art washes away from the soul the dust from everyday life." Having said that, it's intriguing that we are in a political climate that strives to deny particular histories and historical events, and books are being banned to accomplish that end. So, perhaps art images can help counter that as repositories of truth and history. Historically, images have been used to promote false narratives and create harmful government policies such as anti-immigrant legislation—and, at the same time, images have triggered lasting social justice movements.

The relationship between artists and the church was at one time symbiotic. Artists were commissioned to create images that offered early Christians a way to understand biblical stories, scripture, and theology. The arts served a communal function and were integrated into church life. Images offered beauty and access to transcendence. Divorced from formal institutions, artists today make work that is rooted in a contemplative approach and, as such, is responding to what is happening in the moment. Such art is prophetic and offers a collective process that includes beauty and can invite participation in a particular activity or action. This invitation can raise questions that challenge the audience to unpack complex issues. In this way, artists function as "technicians of the sacred," and they are also healers.

What follows is a discussion of art records, an archive of public-art actions which integrate activism and contemplation through face-to-face encounters.

TRUTH TELLING LEADS TO CONTEMPLATIVE SOLIDARITY

WHEN I DISCOVERED the Center for Action and Contemplation's Living School, I was in the midst of discerning what God might be inviting me to do differently if I allowed myself to be softened by grief after my mother's passing. I've learned that saying yes to God involves grace rather than self-will. I was trying to say yes that Labor Day week after spending the summer immersed in nature's beauty. I had traveled to various breathtaking locations, making art and sketching as a form of pilgrimage. My final destination was an island in Maine known as God's Pocket, where I discovered a deeper spiritual intuition that was guiding me toward a new beginning. When I returned to New York City, I came across a reference to the Living School and decided to apply.

On January 21, 2017, I attended the women's march in Washington, DC. It was life-giving and inspiring. However, this was followed by the new administration's very aggressive anti-immigrant policies, the Muslim ban, and mass detention and deportations at the southern border. Intuitively, I recognized parts of my story in the plight of current immigrants. I recognized an emerging pattern of authoritarianism as the scapegoating of immigrants escalated. My anger gave way to curiosity and inspiration. I began research on a new art project about my parents' experience while living under the dictatorship of Rafael Trujillo (1932–1961) and how his subsequent assassination and the revolution that followed became a catalyst for our own family's separation and eventual migration to New York City from the Dominican Republic.

My parents never spoke about what happened, and I created a "family album" to document the April 1965 US invasion of the

> Similar to our experience of nature, art is the spiritual made tangible.

Dominican Republic in order to reclaim this history. Our family was separated shortly after Lyndon B. Johnson (1908–1973) sent 42,000 Marines into Santo Domingo. Until I began this research, I didn't know my story well enough to feel the impact of my immigrant experience. I made the first images in shock, then anger, which gradually gave way to awe that felt like a new beginning.

It didn't settle anything for me that our time in Ciudad Nueva coincided with the US bombing and occupation of Santo Domingo, so I set out to document history as a way to witness what happened. I made drawings to fixate on something, to clearly capture and digest the past for the first time. The historical drawings became part of my story, which is also a universal story of immigrants forced to flee the instability created by war. This body of work raises questions about the impact of militarism and the cultural price of displacement and migration. US intervention created instability, poverty, and displacement, which led to the vast Dominican diaspora, including formation of the largest immigrant community in New York City.

THE BORDER CROSSED US

As reports of the conditions in the immigrant detention centers were leaked, I was invited to speak at Bryn Mawr College on my art project "Las Mujeres de Abril" (The Women of April) and also to lead an anti-deportation solidarity art-action workshop for students and faculty. During the art action, I gave them three prompts. In the first, they were asked to consider what they would pack if faced with deportation. They were asked to design a suitcase that would either contain something to comfort them and keep them safe or that contained a memento to remind them of the life and people they were leaving behind.

Because US immigration is always about defining American identity and who does or does not get to claim that, the second art action asked them to consider American identity. Using the phrase "The border crossed us" to detach "nationality" from "belonging," I asked them to imagine and create a passport that expanded the notion of identity when it is not tied to nationality. In this way, the nation of origin would not be a barrier for movement to another nation. The students reconsidered notions of identity and how it can be designated in ways that recognize our humanity. This created a contemplative space to consider what is actually essential to know about "the other."

PAINTED PRAYERS

ANOTHER ART ACTION with a spiritual component is known as "artivism," which uses art as an activist practice which may or may not be political. The art action which most impacted and transformed me was the installation "Please Take One: Free Love, Compassion, and Gratitude" that I created at a church in New York City. I filled a large metal bowl with small paintings, each with an intention written on the back. The installation was an invitation to parishioners and all church visitors to engage in face-to-face transmission. One of three intentions was written on the back of each painting, and they were asked to take a painting and give it away as gratitude, love, or compassion to a stranger, a loved one, or to themselves. Making the installation was also a contemplative act which allowed me to call forth more compassion, love, and gratitude as I made each work during a period when I felt myself needing all three. The installation was set up in June, during pride month in New York City, and close to 800 small "painted prayers" and intentions were given away that month.

> As I made art, I experienced time as stillness, and its slowness transformed my artwork.

IRREVOCABLY BEAUTIFUL

Someone recently shared that Christianity challenges the status quo because it fosters the right to resist. This is the simplest throughline for the work I have been making the last few years, in spite of backing into Christianity during a lengthy spiritual search which unfolded over an equally lengthy period of caregiving. When caregiving ended, what remained—along with the love and shared memories—was a visual archive of the caregiving journey during which Mom was my muse.

I created over 300 paintings and drawings which document the many twists and turns of that ten-year period. During this time, I used my art to witness and to archive our moments together. Artmaking was a way of spending time with Mom. As I made art, I experienced time as stillness, and its slowness transformed my artwork. My art became more intimate and thoughtful, and, though I was unaware of this then, my creativity flourished in ways that altered what I choose to create and share with audiences today. That contemplative time of suffering and paying attention transformed me as much as it transformed my work, allowing me to use art as a form of reportage and witnessing, and to engage in face-to-face transmission. •

The Ascension of Christ, Hans Süss von Kulmbach (1480–1522), 1513, oil on fir, painted surface 24 1/4 x 14 1/8 in. Rogers Fund, 1921. Accession Number: 21.84. Metropolitan museum of Art. Public domain.

The Artist's Access to Mystery

By Richard Rohr

ART AND SPIRITUALITY

THERE MUST BE a way to be both *here* and in the *depth of here*. Jesus is the here, Christ is the depth of here. This, in my mind, is the essence of incarnation, and the gift of contemplation. We must learn to love and enjoy things as they are, in their depth, in their soul, and in their fullness. Contemplation is the "second gaze," through which we see something in its particularity and yet also in a much larger frame. We know it by the joy it gives, which is far greater than anything it does for us in terms of money, power, or success.

Two pieces of art have given me this incarnational and contemplative insight. The first was one I saw in a Nuremberg art museum by Hans von Kulmbach (c. 1480–1522).[1] It portrays the two human feet of Jesus at the very top of a large painting of the Ascension. Most of the canvas is taken up by the apostles, who are drawn up with Christ through their eyes, as his feet move off the top of the painting, presumably into the spiritual realms. The image had a wonderful effect on me. I too found myself looking beyond the painting toward the ceiling of the art museum, my eyes drawn elsewhere for the message. It was a mystical moment—one that simultaneously took me beyond the painting and right back into the room where I was standing. It was an instance of understanding the Christ in a collective sense, not just his ascension but also ours. Read texts like Colossians 2:11–15 and Ephesians 2:4–6 and notice how they clearly present salvation in both the past tense and the collective sense. Why did we never notice this?

The second piece of art is a small bronze statue of St. Francis, located in the upper basilica of Assisi, Italy. Created by a sculptor whose name is hidden, the statue shows Francis gazing down into the dirt with awe and wonder, which is quite unusual and almost shocking. The Holy Spirit, who is almost always pictured as descending from above, is pictured here as coming from below—even to the point of being hidden in the dirt! I've made sure to go see this statue whenever I return to Assisi, but I fear most people miss it, because it is small and set off to the side—just like the Christ message itself. "Truly, you are a hidden God," Isaiah said (45:15). God is hidden in the dirt and mud instead of descending from the clouds. This is a major transposition of place. Once we know that the miracle of "Word made flesh" has become the very nature of the universe, we cannot help but be both happy and holy. What we first of all need is here!

It was a mystical moment—
one that simultaneously
took me beyond
the painting…

Both these pieces of art put the two worlds together, but from different perspectives. Yet in both images, *it is the Divine that takes the lead in changing places*. Maybe artists have easier access to this Mystery than many theologians? The right brain often gets there faster and more easily than the left brain, and we let the left brainers take over our churches. I doubt if we can see the image of God (*Imago Dei*) in our fellow humans if we cannot first see it in rudimentary form in stones, in plants and flowers, in strange little animals, in bread and wine, and most especially cannot honor this objective divine image in ourselves. It is a full-body tune-up, this spiritual journey. It really ends up being *all or nothing, here and then everywhere*.[2] •

…and right
back into the room
where I was standing.

The Art of Food

By Felicia Murrell

FOOD WAS A highlight of our life in Washington, DC, especially eating crabs. My grandparents would go down to some place in Southeast, off Branch Avenue, and buy a bushel or two of live crabs. We'd take those crabs back to Grandma and Granddaddy's place, and Grandma would pull out this gigantic lobster pot. Granddaddy would pour a six pack of beer in the pot with some Old Bay seasoning, add some water, and set the pot to boil. Then my brother and I would clamber over each other, trying to watch the crabs crawl to their death in the pot. And while we were in the kitchen with Granddaddy, watching the crabs turn magical in the pot, Grandma would be in the dining room, spreading newspaper for our feast. Once we were folded into dining chairs, she taught us how to identify the dead man and told us not to eat the mustard, all while slipping her German Shepherd, Rex, pieces of crab meat.

I think about artists like Hale Woodruff and Ayana Ross, photographers like Gordon Parks and Montinique Monroe, ones who specialize in lifestyle photography, realism, and photojournalism. How might they have captured my Gram's Formica table? What elements of my grandparents' home would they highlight in the background? What colors on their palette would they swirl about their paintbrush to mimic the framed picture of dogs playing poker centered just so on the wood paneling behind the table? What aperture of the camera lens would be necessary to capture the bend of the black leatherette-wrapped counter-height bar off to the right of my grandparents' Formica table?

And that returns me to food. Food is a thread that weaves the fabric of our universe together. We all have to eat to stay alive. What we eat, when we eat, and how we eat differ greatly, but the act of eating—consuming food to remain a part of this breathing, living, energetic tapestry we call humanity—is a common practice we all share.

> *This ritual is One. The food is One. We who offer the food are One. The fire of hunger is also One. All action is One. We who understand this are One.*
> —Hindu blessing, Bhagavad Gita

IN A WORLD of privilege, food is a conduit for memories and merrymaking. In our home, food serves as a vehicle for connection. And like at my grandparents' home so long ago, the place where we commune is the table. There, we linger, long after food has been consumed. For our family, food is a gathering point. Amongst a spread of dishes, we guide each other with the love in our eyes. We share about our day, tell of things we found funny, speak softly of hard places and points of frustration. Vulnerable mutuality is expelled like currents of energy in the rise and fall of hand to mouth, the reciprocity of back and forth, give and take.

Amid the clinking of forks, in the silence of our breathing, food and life go together. Bleeding over and into one another, food sustains life. Life is fed to one another as a kind of holy eucharist, giving and sharing ourselves—our highs, our lows, our joys, our sorrows—emptying our lives into one another through conversation and laughter, deep sighs of camaraderie and audible moans of utter delight.

Isn't that so like art? Art is a vehicle for connection. Paintings, photographs, and sculptures tell of things we find funny. Artists capture in

> Like literature, food weaves a story about place, seeds, the soil, the harvester, the laborer, the truck driver, the animal, the cook.

magnificent ways the hard places, points of frustration, and even the mundanity and awe of our day-to-day existence. Vulnerable mutuality is expelled in swirls of paint and skill onto canvas, metal, ceramics, sides of buildings, and other mediums. The artist is giving and sharing of themselves, emptying their hearts, becoming the lens through which they interpret life out onto canvasses for our consumption, our enjoyment, our critique.

I think of how art makes me feel: sometimes light, so free I could fly and soar; other times heavy, weighed down by the story I've created as I consumed an artist's work. And then I think of food as art, how this feeling of lightness or heaviness also mimics the way I feel with food.

Like literature, food weaves a story about place, seeds, the soil, the harvester, the laborer, the truck driver, the animal, the cook. Sometimes, food tells a story about home or longing—the missing. Sometimes, food as language tells a story about safety or harm. Like all things in humanity, it's easy to pervert that which is sacred, profaning what Creator deemed *good* with toxins, additives, hormones, and pesticides.

As with art, I'm invited to consider my relationship with food. Am I maintaining integrity with the environment, with myself and my spiritual practice, in my relationship with food? What is the story I tell myself when I choose certain foods? How am I interpreting the world around me through my food consumption?

I want food to heal and not harm, to empower, to strengthen and renew, to lead to life. In this way, I see food like art, food as art. I'm thinking of art therapy, how it heals. The way art pulls people out of their problems. The way art invites us to lose ourselves in exploration and imagination. The way art expands our hearts and engages the use of our limbs, our senses. What story might food be inviting us into? How might thinking of food as art lead to a more contemplative relationship with food?

I'M GRATEFUL FOR food. Almost all my most cherished memories are anchored in some way to food. Food makes me happy. I love its colors. I love its vibrancy. I love its sustainability. I love its comfort. I love the way food brings people together.

Like art, food removes the distance between us. Food shrinks the chasm between cultural divides, offering us a way to experience and learn about other cultures. Food tells a story. Food affords us an opportunity to learn about cultural experiences different than our own. Food, like art with its varied expressions—gothic, renaissance, baroque, romantic, modern—holds space for proclivity of taste, familiarity, and preference while throwing its arms wide open to a bounty of cuisines flavored by distinct cultural and individual expressions. Search #jollofrice on X, formerly known as Twitter, and note all the varied expressions of this one staple across cultures of the global African diaspora. While we may not always agree on how to prepare it, food is an easy entry point to the practice of inclusion. The table is one place where we don't hesitate to make room, smiling as we scoot closer together for more people to fit. The people we eat with, the laughter, and the conversation remain in our hearts long after the food is cleared from the table.

The consumption of food is the singular event where we all pause and embrace the shared act of communing, even if we are only pausing to commune with ourselves. Food, like art, is a link to common union—the embrace of all humanity in the communion of our personhood.

T HE RADICAL GENEROSITY and brave vulnerability of chef and artist alike are gifted to us through the kenotic process of creating: emptying themselves, their ingenuity and creativity, into paint or plate, whatever their medium may be.

How are we, those of us who bear witness as participants and patrons, being invited into our own kenotic process? How do we engage with food as a means for transformation—for our world, for our own bodies—and how does the art of food participate in our transformation? What captures our eye?

Engaging with beauty gentles me. I want to name the beauty and, thinking of oppressed, indigent, and impoverished populations who may never experience a leisurely jaunt through the halls of an art museum or feast at the table of a fine-dining establishment, I want to name the privilege of knowing the beauty of food, beyond a means for survival and being exposed to art. In today's economy, beautiful food is expensive. Acknowledging this, I understand that for some, the exorbitance of white-tablecloth dining is a turnoff, the idea marred by cynicism.

"What you eat represents your social status, not your love. The poor eat to end their hunger. But when you can buy more food, your hunger doesn't end. You hunger for approval, something special, exclusive experiences."[1] I hunger for love, for the wellness of humanity, for our safety and peace. I also hunger for beauty, for awe, for wonder. The artistry of food plating captures my eye.

My food Instagram page (@FetheFoodie) attests to this. I turned fifty in 2022, and my husband Doug gifted me dinner on Chicago's West Loop at Chef Curtis Duffy's famed two-star Michelin restaurant, Ever. That night, I wanted to be in the moment. To savor the beauty of each presentation. To smell each culinary delight. To close my eyes and sear into my memory the tastes that lingered on my palate. And, I needed a photo of each dish so I wouldn't forget the extraordinary experience! Months after dining at Ever, whenever I recalled a dish or smell, a phantom taste would emerge in my mind. I'm struck by how similar this feels to the way my heart explodes when I think of the artistry of Yayoi Kusama, Kehinde Wiley, or Johannes Vermeer's *Girl with a Pearl Earring*.

For two and a half hours, Chef Duffy and his team delivered course after course with immaculately timed synchronization. In one particular course, we were served an amber liquid in a crystal goblet with an opaque spherical bubble rising from the glass. As an art curator would do for any piece they're explaining, the server introduced the dish and then instructed us to tap the bubble with a knife before sipping from the glass.

Your eye expects a drink, an interlude between food courses. What we were not prepared for was the most heavenly meaty aroma (with apologies to my vegetarian and vegan friends) that emitted when we popped the bubble, and then for the glass to be filled with a delicious, warm, comforting bone broth that even now evokes a feeling akin to a deep hug.

Like any artist, a good chef knows that we eat with our eyes first. Artists invite us into their worlds visually. The vibrancy and poignancy of their renderings lower our defenses, creating a vulnerability for us to receive the message they want to convey through their art.

With food, the plate is the chef's canvas. How, why, and what a chef chooses to plate, and even the chosen vessel are expressions of their creativity. The intentionality and thought behind each placement are a journey into the chef's artistry. For a chef or even a home cook who is participating with food as a vehicle to create connection and nourishment for their family; the sacred act of choice and attention to details in selecting key ingredients, ensuring balance, and creating a framework upon which to place the portion of food that will be served; the alchemy of fire that turns fresh produce, spices, herbs, and raw meat into culinary wonders—all are a part of the transformative process of food as art.

> The alchemy of fire that turns fresh produce, spices, herbs, and raw meat into culinary wonders—all are a part of the transformative process of food as art.

At first glance, the art of food plating may give off an air of perfectionism, which lends itself to the illusion of order and control. But, when I think of art and the artist, how an artist visualizes a concept; creates a structure, a framework to bring to life what they envision in their mind's eye; and then revises and edits their project before landing on the finished product (whether home cook or professional chef), the one in the kitchen walks a similar path: beginning with a concept in their head, bringing the ingredients together, creating the recipe, revising, editing, adding this or that, and then, moving their finished product onto a surface to share it with their family or their patrons.

With a long, loving, contemplative gaze, I'm invited to explore with the art of food plating similar things that I find evocative about gallery art. What colors and food types does the chef choose to pair together and why? What of the food-plating style speaks to me? Upon first glance at a plate, what does it call forth? What awakens in me as I observe this food on the plate? What does the chef hope the patron will see? What story is the chef telling me through this food? How is it interpreted once it's on the plate? What emotions arise as I take in this food with my eyes, with my olfactory senses? What memory does the food recall when I taste it? What memory of the cook was tied to their envisioning of this dish, from pot to plate? How am I being invited to honor the labor of love woven into this chef's story and process?

What does thinking about the art of food invite us to consider beyond merely eating to live—or its gluttonous counterpart, living to eat? When I partake of food, consciously and with intent, I am being invited to participate in humanity's mycelial network. Food, like art, carries an energetic resonance that deepens our shared humanity. •

Joshua: 45-46

By Josh Radnor

I RECENTLY RELEASED THE first volume of a double album I recorded in Nashville in 2022. It's titled (fittingly) *Eulogy*, as each song, in its own way, is a kind of mini funeral for parts of myself that were once vital and necessary but have outlived their usefulness. Rather than giving them a pauper's burial, I decided to honor and memorialize these former selves in song before laying them to rest—a farewell to the first half of life and a benediction for the second. *Where have I been? What have I learned? Where am I now? Where am I headed?*

The memory of these past selves can cause me to blush or wince, but I've come to feel they're deserving of my compassion. They did their best with the tools they had at the time and got me to the other side of multiple rivers. There I could then, as the Buddhists advise, drop the canoe.

The final song on the first volume is called "Joshua: 45-46." I love that it looks like a Bible verse, but it's really a song I wrote to myself as my forty-sixth birthday approached. My back had gone out, and I was feeling low. I sometimes write songs as prayers or pep talks to myself, to allow something wiser and kinder than my egoic mind to take over and whisper truths to me. And if the song has a strong heartbeat, I end up playing it for years and get to hear that good advice to myself over and over.

I went to Hebrew day school from kindergarten through eighth grade. My youth was saturated with stories from the Torah. I continue to love sacred literature, even as my appetites have expanded beyond the borders of my tradition. I have a strong distaste for arguments about the literal veracity of the Bible. It feels very much beside the point. As Reza Aslan has said, sacred history and actual history are different. That doesn't mean sacred history is any less true. Was there a man named Joshua who marched his army around the city of Jericho for six straight days, with the high priests blowing rams' horns, resulting in the walls of the city crumbling on the seventh day? I have no idea, and it doesn't much matter to me. What matters is the notion of walls coming down: that with patience and divine assistance, we can dissolve borders, barriers, and stuckness.

The song—a sort of midlife reckoning—covers a lot of ground in a short time: the vertigo caused by the passing of time; the rigors of aging offset by the joy of writing music and playing guitar; the blessing and the wounds left by playing a character on TV for nine years of my life, something that has liberated and imprisoned me in equal measure; the self-consciousness inspired by people's opinions and projections. But it doesn't stay in turmoil. There's a release, an un-gripping, a forgiveness that takes place.

(I joke that this is the one song of mine that is so autobiographical it would be really hard to cover. And, as far as I know, it's the only song that makes oblique references to Ted Mosby from *How I Met Your Mother*, Julian of Norwich, and St. Teresa of Ávila.)

I so appreciate Richard Rohr's gorgeous teaching that the Bible doesn't begin with Genesis 3:1 and the Fall. It begins at 1:1, with God declaring over and over that God's creation is *good*. Not original sin, original blessing. This merciful teaching is the antidote to shame. At the core of the core of the core of us are not wretchedness, rottenness, and sin, but rather love, benevolence, mercy, and grace.

So, this song is a prayer of thanks to God, to stories, to teachers, to music, to time, and to my younger selves that got me to middle age: wounded, imperfect, and immeasurably grateful.

Joshua: 45-46

You feel like you are seventeen
Your back says you are forty-five
At least it does this morning
You've lost the kicks from your old tricks
In a week you will be forty-six
The birthdays come without warning

How did I get so old?
I'm not really old but I'm no longer young
And now I'm playing this guitar
It feels so good to sing, my fingers on these strings

And I get stopped in airports because I played an architect
Some people think that's who I am
It used to drive me crazy and some days it still does
But I'm learning how not to give a damn

What do they think of me?
What a waste of time, I've wasted so much time
With all those years of walking blind
I was hypnotized, mud upon my eyes

Oh Joshua
He made a mighty sound and the walls came tumbling down
In old Jericho
And now I bear his name and I'm doing the same
The walls are coming down

I started writing songs when I was just north of forty
I try to write some every day
I wish that I had started sometime in the nineties but I'm not sure
    I had much to say

Oh with my Leo sun Sagittarian moon born late afternoon
With all that fire in my chest I have had to learn how not to get
    burned

And Richard says that God is love
I'm starting to believe him
I can feel it in the mountains and the water in the air
And Julian said that all is well
Teresa said, "There is a hell . . .
It's just that no one's there."

I know it's good to be alive
It's good to have a body
It's good to have a mind
And I . . . I'm done with right and wrong
God is not a test but arms where I can rest

Oh Joshua, He made mighty sound and the walls came tumbling down
In old Jericho and now I bear his name and I'm doing the same
Oh Joshua, he made mighty sound and the walls came tumbling down
In old Jericho and now I bear his name and I'm doing the same
Oh Joshua, he made a mighty sound and the walls came tumbling down
Oh Joshua, he made a mighty sound and the walls came tumbling down
Oh Joshua, he made a mighty sound and the walls came tumbling down
Oh Joshua, he made a mighty sound and the walls came tumbling down
Oh Joshua, he made a mighty sound and the walls came tumbling down
Oh Joshua, he made a mighty sound and the walls came tumbling down
In old, in old Jericho and now I bear his name and I'm doing the same.[1]

Arroyo Hondo Reredo, Marie Romero Cash, 1985, 27 x 25 in., Santa Maria de la Vid Abbey, NM. Used with permission.

Discovering My Soul

By Marie Romero Cash

To send light into the darkness of men's hearts—such is the duty of the artist.
—Robert Schumann

ART AND SPIRITUALITY
51

THE RELATIONSHIP BETWEEN art and spirituality can be a difficult one to define. These are two domains that for all time have been connected to the human experience. On the one hand, art is the product of creativity. On the other hand, spirituality can be infused into art based on the artist's intentions and beliefs. The process can be intentional or subconscious.

In my own work, I believe that my creations are powered by something higher than myself. I didn't set out to be labeled a spiritual or sacred artist, but somewhere along the way, I garnered the title of *Santera*, a maker of religious images.

Each culture has its beliefs, but one thing that is similar in most is the *idea* of a spirituality based on these beliefs. A culture's art plays an integral part in worship and devotion and serves to create a sacred space, evoke an emotion, or convey a subtle message to the viewer. In most instances, spiritual art is very personal. In others, it serves to transmit a social critique, where symbols reflecting the artist's beliefs are incorporated either subtly or blatantly.

Some individuals might believe they are more spiritual than religious. Do those two go hand in hand? Can one be spiritual and not religious, and vice versa? Religion and spirituality include belief in something beyond the self. So, for me, it is logical to create both spiritual and religious images.

I am most at peace when in my studio. The world outside blurs, and I am transported to a place of calm and quietude as I carve or paint. I have often said that my pieces come alive when I apply paint to the faces. Until then, they are but figments of my imagination and have not yet moved into being.

As a combination of my religion and my spirituality, when in the process of creating what I consider to be a holy or sacred image, I will sometimes use holy water as the vehicle for watercolor. From my perspective, this infuses the painting with a certain intensity unseen by the naked eye.

I strive for my art to evoke a sense of calming depth. This was instrumental when I was commissioned to create Stations of the Cross for the Cathedral Basilica of St. Francis of Assisi in Santa Fe, New Mexico. The fifteen panels would be housed in a place of worship and ultimately seen by thousands of parishioners and tourists. It was humbling to realize that I had created art that would serve as a reminder of Jesus' passion, but also that the art itself would be viewed with awe and wonder. I wanted the paintings to evoke a sense of spirituality.

Throughout an art career spanning almost half a century, I have considered my work to be spiritual, not religious. When someone would express that they loved my work, but they weren't Catholic, I would respond that my work is folk art, not religious art, as that is how I perceived it. So, how could I believe that a spiritually induced religious image might be such an oxymoron? Again, it is because a great percentage of my art is based on religion but created through spirituality.

I read somewhere that a painting of the crucifixion by a painter who does not believe in Jesus might not be able to produce an emotion from the observer. I have often been humbled when walking through the Cathedral Basilica in Santa Fe as I observed someone deep in prayer while looking up to one of the Stations of the Cross which I created. At other times, I have been a witness to my more colorful contemporary works of art evoking joyful emotions from both children and adults, their eyes lighting up as they view an ark with numerous pairs of carved and painted animals being herded aboard by Noah, or a revolving staircase housing multiple sculptures of vibrantly colored "bad girls" of the Bible.

In conversations with artists who create religious art, I was not surprised to learn that many of them are of the opinion that the icons they create come from an inner space, sometimes outside their understanding. I also hold that belief. It's not always about financial gain. Yes, as artists, we need to make a living, but it's more about transferring an image from the mind to the canvas and being moved to add paint and color shading until the painting has evolved into or beyond its original concept.

My parents were traditional New Mexican tinsmiths who used historical examples of tinwork as a basis for their creations. On many occasions, my father urged me to begin and end each day by expressing gratitude to the Holy Spirit for the inspiration to create beautiful and wonderful images in its honor, a practice I have become accustomed to over the decades. It is how I begin and end each day that I am fortunate enough to be given.

Creating art, no matter what genre, can transport one into another realm, where time stands still, and random thoughts cease. It can also become a vessel by which spirituality can be injected into the canvas as one searches for the meaning and value of their work, thus allowing one to transcend limitations, celebrate an unknown potential, and overcome life's challenges.

A study conducted by the Pew Research Center concluded that the religious commitment of men and women differs due to a combination of socialization, personality, and biology.[1] I believe that as children we are immersed into the religion of our parents, and, throughout life, we are taught and encouraged to follow these early teachings. My Catholic upbringing engrained many aspects of the tradition into my psyche, because I and my six siblings had an inordinate number of rules and regulations pounded into us. We each grew up to be spiritual in our own ways, but with some of us abandoning certain religious aspects of those early teachings. As we became aware of other world religions, we learned that each held many of the same values as Catholicism, just presented with a different perspective.

Each of the seven children in our family was artistic, some more than others. I imagine it was because as we each departed from the family nest (and our parents were freed to pursue their own artistic endeavors, becoming award-winning, nationally recognized crafts persons), we also were freed to pursue whatever life offered. It has become evident that our gene pool contained this ability to create different art forms, which have included tinwork, metal sculpture, woodcarving, *retablo* painting, and traditional New Mexican stitchery.

In my own work, the shift from religious to spiritual art was subtle. Although early on I was commissioned to create large altar screens for historic churches in Northern New Mexico, it was my spiritual nature that supported me in accomplishing the projects—and, although perhaps not visible, that was a necessary ingredient.

I also found this to be true in my research on the early New Mexican *Santeros*. The earliest colonists to New Mexico brought with them few religious items other than those easily carried in a satchel or wrapped in a shawl. Missionization by the Franciscans began the moment they set foot on our soil. Their primary aim was the salvation of souls. Churches and missions were established during those early years. On the high desert plateau nestled between the valleys of the Sangre de Cristo Mountains, villages of varying populations emerged, creating a chain of settlements described in early writings as being spread out like beads on a rosary along the high road from

> As artists, we are visual musicians who create harmony through the images we place on different surfaces. That, to me, is spirituality at its highest level.

Santa Fe to Taos, where early churches were built from adobe bricks made from earth mixed with sand, straw, and water. Once completed, these churches lacked decoration. How could parishioners be expected to worship in a building with only pews, benches, and bare walls?

Religion had traveled easily with these early settlers, as worn rosary beads made the trip in the pockets of farmers who walked next to their cattle and in the kerchiefs of women who wrapped them after each use and placed them safely between their breasts. Once communities were established and churches built, it became more comfortable to practice one's faith. The four walls of the church held the glue to bind the faith of the people together. In hardship and in happiness, the first thing they turned to was prayer. The church was a part of each celebration, from birth to death. It was something on which the people could rely.

It was then that local artisans, with little training in creating religious images, were recruited by Franciscan priests to create paintings and wooden sculptures, however crude, to decorate the churches. An artistic tradition was born of necessity. This tradition was so unique that it would flourish for 150 years and then slowly die out. The art of the New Mexican *Santero* was expressed in three specific ways, through (1) *retablos* or devotional images painted on small wooden panels, (2) *bultos* or three-dimensional images of saints carved from cottonwood and pine, and (3) *reredos* or large, multi-paneled wooden altar screens, each covered with a layer of gesso made from gypsum and then painted with pigments made from locally gathered minerals and plants.

One can easily surmise that these early settlers were highly religious, and the artists commissioned to create art for the newly constructed churches imbued their art with spirituality. It is what they knew. They could not have created paintings and polychromed sculptures of their patron saints without being spiritual in nature. Today, in every museum and private collection, the viewer can see deep into the eyes of the images and know for certain that the maker combined their religion and spirituality into the art before them.

Spirituality is a personal concept. I can't speak for others, but in my own experience, my art has been infused with spirituality or its essence. When one of my brothers was diagnosed with stage IV cancer, I needed a respite from the daily tasks related to his care, which overwhelmed us both. It was then that I began to paint on canvas, a process theretofore unknown to me. Without effort, many images flowed through my hands onto the canvas, including abstract angels with flowing wings and tiny hearts surrounded by symbols from many sources, including Native American, East Coast, and Hispanic symbolism, along with petroglyphs and the extraterrestrial.

During the months of his treatment and up to the time of his passing, I filled my studio with over three dozen paintings. Now, when I look at them, I cannot imagine what energy was being transmitted from somewhere far beyond me. I have tried to duplicate these paintings, but that process no longer exists. It came about from a great need to understand and believe that things would turn out all right. I liken creating that body of art to discovering my soul.

Can someone call themselves a sacred artist as they strive to create seemingly religious images? One of the definitions of the word "spiritual," according to Merriam-Webster, is "of or relating to sacred matters." Would it be better to call spiritual art sacred art? Spirituality is not necessarily connected with a specific religious tradition, but it is an expression (or recognition) of the existence of an inner life which comes to the surface as an artist begins the process of creating.

As artists, we are visual musicians who create harmony through the images we place on different surfaces. That, to me, is spirituality at its highest level. It is as though one is discovering their soul, a purpose for existence. ◆

With New Eyes

By Catherine Dowling

My love affair with the United States began when I was eight. It didn't take much, just a couple of black-and-white photos that I found at the bottom of a wardrobe. One image was of my father's aunts, Bridget and Elizabeth, taken in the 1930s. They had emigrated from Ireland to Amsterdam, New York, a mill town on the sloping banks of the Mohawk River. Smiling, slightly portly women, they stood in front of a row of brick houses with big windows and steps up to the front door. They wore hats, and white gloves, and linked arms in the dappled sunshine. The other photo was of Elizabeth's son, Willis. He was dressed in a Boy Scout uniform of shorts and a shirt, yet he stood ankle deep in pristine snow that sparkled in the sunlight. Those photos told me all I needed to know—in America, the sun always shone, snow wasn't cold, everyone lived in big houses with freshly painted porches, all families were happy, and that damp-fed moss that crept over everything in Ireland was nowhere to be found. I was smitten.

When my family got a television set, America came to life in our living room. Through shows and films that were decades out of date in the US, I learned that America wasn't just clean and bright; it was free. In Ireland, a woman's primary duty as a homemaker was enshrined in the constitution. Poverty and the Catholic church kept everything closed in and battened down; life seemed suffocating, particularly for women. But, on the other side of the Atlantic, plucky, beautiful Jean Arthur, my favorite actress (who grew up not too far from Amsterdam), barged her way through her celluloid world afraid of no man. There were no walls she couldn't climb—in a beautifully tailored suit with matching hat. James Stewart's Mr. Smith went to Washington to fight for the rights of poor people, and he won because, in America, good always triumphed over evil, and even poor people wore clothes that fit.

Later, a darker side of the United States filtered through. Ireland's only radio station played Pete Seeger and Woody Guthrie—the music of social justice. Kent State, hippies, and the magnificent Angela Davis filled the news, right after coverage of the daily bombings and shootings in Northern Ireland, sixty miles away. On TV, I watched grainy images of civil rights protests in the deep South, of sit-ins and bodies crushed by the force of water from fire hoses. On the Edmund Pettus Bridge, unarmed marchers dressed for church were bludgeoned by white state troopers. But President Johnson took a righteous stand. The Voting Rights Act followed. And in 1976, as I took a seat on my first ever flight to the United States, black Americans seemed to have achieved equality, something Catholics in Northern Ireland would not get for another twenty-three years.

So, IN JUNE of America's bicentennial year, I stepped down from a Greyhound bus into what was once the vacation capital of the United States: Atlantic City, New Jersey. I had just turned twenty-one. 1976 was the year when Americans wished each other happy birthday, the year Jimmy Carter was elected president, and the year Atlantic City legalized gambling. It was eight years before Donald Trump opened his first casino on the Boardwalk.

I had an address of a boarding house on St. James Place, and as I wandered through town without a map, I could feel a tangible sense of possibility. It was there in the crystal light, the same light that dappled the black-and-white photos of my great aunts and glowed from the Jean Arthur movies that I loved. It was in the sea air, in the bright summer clothes everyone wore, in the shops I passed where people bought so many things without, it seemed, considering the price of anything. Possibility of what? It never occurred to me to ask. It didn't matter. It was enough to know that at last there was possibility.

"Get outta my neighborhood!" a woman yelled from above.

I had stopped to rest beside a yellow-brick building. On the top floor, a black face framed by Angela Davis hair leaned out the only open window. She looked straight at me.

"Go back where you belong," she yelled again, then slammed the window shut.

My first thought was that I must have done something wrong, broken some American rule I didn't know existed. Was she calling the police right then? Panic bloomed in my stomach. Maybe I should never have come here? But I was lost, and overheated, and the straps of my orange backpack were cutting into my shoulders. Pain brought focus. I spotted a boxy looking restaurant beneath towering yellow arches and headed toward it. Surely someone there could give me directions.

St. James Place, it turned out, was only a few blocks away. A short street sandwiched between New York Avenue to the south and Tennessee to the north, it was lined with multi-story boarding houses in shades of yellow and cream. The ground floor of each house abutted the footpath, the floors above further back so that the roof of the ground floor became a large, railed porch. Here and there on the porches, people sat in groups, smoking, talking, playing cards. They were mostly older people, boarding house managers or owners perhaps, waiting for the summer season to begin. I climbed the stairs of one of the houses and asked if they had any vacancies.

"Where're you from?" one of the women asked. Her skin seemed excessively wrinkled, her lacquer-rigid hair too dark for her age. I would later learn the bright, shapeless dress she wore was called a muumuu. Definitely not Jean Arthur. She was the house manager and yes, she had vacancies. I paid for a week in advance and hauled my backpack up to a tiny room with a view of the side of the house next door. In the next couple of weeks, the boarding house would fill up with Irish students, many of whom I knew from college.

"Can you waitress?" the manager asked me that evening. I'd worked "below stairs" in a well-known Dublin restaurant, Bewley's Oriental Café. In Bewley's, you had to work your way up the hierarchy to waitressing. I washed dishes, scrubbed floors, and broke an inordinate number of plates, but I never got anywhere near server status.

"Yes," I replied, "I can waitress." She advised me to get up early the next day and go door to door on the Boardwalk—just walk in and ask for a job.

St. James Place and New York and Tennessee Avenues were the orange streets on the original Monopoly board, valued at $180 each. At the eastern end of St. James Place, ramps lead up to the Boardwalk—at $400, the most expensive street in Monopoly. The Boardwalk's wooden thoroughfare runs the entire length of Atlantic City's coastline, the boards laid out in an attractive herringbone pattern. On its eastern side, beyond a wide, sandy beach, the Atlantic Ocean stretches, sometimes grey, sometimes blue, to the horizon.

That was where, the next morning, I began my job search. Because I found it so difficult to just walk into a place and ask for work, I was easily distracted by everything around me. Many of the old hotels were still there. I took my time admiring the redbrick Claridge where Marilyn Monroe once stayed and the Marlborough-Blenheim where Winston Churchill resided when he was in town. Domed, turreted, towered, some capped with precipitously sloping roofs, I could see how the Boardwalk once lived up to its premier position on the Monopoly board.

I tried to imagine what it must have been like twenty, thirty, fifty years earlier: Elegant women in floaty sundresses and matching shoes, arm in arm with handsome young men, their hair neatly cut, buying ice creams, salt-water taffy, and tickets to the amusements on the piers that jutted out into the Atlantic. But I didn't see anyone like that. The people strolling by were often overweight and wore shorts, t-shirts, and cheap flip-flops. Some shop fronts were still delightfully old fashioned, with striped awnings and a distinct Art Deco vibe, but most traded beneath plastic signs in garish red and yellow. A dizzying array of souvenirs, beachwear, postcards, and taffy spilled out onto the wooden boardwalk. Everything looked tired—in need of fresh paint, perhaps, or fewer plastic signs. But jaded as it was, I loved this worn-out piece of the country that had captured my imagination since childhood.

A couple of hours later, I stopped in front of a five-story pale-colored building on the corner of Ocean Avenue. Above the sheet-glass windows of the ground floor, the word Woolworth's stretched in huge red letters across a white tile background. That was a name I recognized. There were two Woolworth's in Dublin. My mother once took me and my brothers out to eat in Woolworth's cafeteria, a rare and special treat. If Woolworth's in Dublin had a cafeteria, surely the one in Atlantic City did too.

Familiarity gave me courage. I pushed through the glass doors into a cavern full of everything from a needle and thread to beach supplies and cosmetics. The cafeteria at the back of the shop was quite an elegant affair as cafeterias go, with neat little tables surrounded by matching metal-framed chairs. I asked to speak to the manager. Minutes later, a handsome black man in a dark suit, not much taller than my five foot four, approached me. His manner was gentle, but businesslike, maybe a little harried.

"Can you waitress?" he asked.

"Of course," I said. As with the house manager the day before, it wasn't really a lie. He asked *can* I waitress, not *had* I. And with that, I was hired, to start the next day, no references, no demands to see my visa. In the neighborhood I came from in Dublin, unemployment hovered around 40 percent. I knew people who had searched for months, even years for work. In Atlantic City, it took me a couple of hours to get a job. The rumors were true: In America, jobs grew on trees.

> "Can you waitress?" he asked.
> "Of course," I said.

My job at Woolworth's wasn't really waitressing. I dished out hot food to the customers lining up for breakfast or lunch and helped keep the food counter stocked. On my second day, when I went to the kitchen for a fresh tray of scrambled eggs, I found out the eggs didn't come from white or brown shells cracked open and whisked together. They flowed in a pale-yellow stream from a carton. I found the discovery mildly disturbing and made a mental note not to eat eggs in Woolworth's.

The cafeteria went through a surprisingly large amount of fresh fruit, which led to another discovery—a huge walk-in refrigerator packed with boxes of melons, apples, grapes, oranges, and strawberries. Always there were strawberries, red and plump at the peak of ripeness. The temptation was too much. Every time I went to the fridge to replenish the fruit on the counter, I ate a few. I wasn't the only one. As the days passed, I met staff from different departments— dishwashers, cashiers, shop assistants—all in the fridge, all surreptitiously nibbling strawberries.

Over time, we began to talk, snatching conversations as furtively as we snatched fruit until the sound of an approaching manager sent us scrambling for the door. It was there, in Woolworth's fridge, that I began to notice the many shades of human skin. Ireland in the 1970s was an almost all-white country, mainly because it was so poor that nobody wanted to move there. The only black people I saw were African doctors interning in Irish hospitals or the popular Phil Lynott, a biracial rock singer with an unruly afro and a cheeky smile. Black and brown people were one-dimensional images in books or on TV. In Woolworth's fridge, they became real.

Jimmy, from Puerto Rico, explained his home to me, an island marooned between statehood and nationhood with none of the advantages of either. Both my parents were white, but year-round my father looked like he'd just returned from intensive sunbathing on the Mediterranean. Jimmy's skin was an almost identical shade of warm, golden-tan. Angela, a Native American, spoke with cushiony softness. Her light skin had a slightly grey undertone, and she talked wistfully about riding in the back of a pickup truck on "the rez" in Arizona. She had run away a year ago, following a boyfriend east, but now she wanted desperately to go home and was working two jobs to save the bus fare. Rich, a New York City native with Greek parents, was almost as pasty white as I. He said he was just passing through Atlantic

City, but he was mysteriously vague about where he would go when summer ended and the jobs dried up. He threw out words in a rapid-fire, high-energy New York way I found mesmerizing. Rochelle was dark brown, from Philadelphia, a student like me, in Atlantic City to earn money. She was laser-focused on law school and could talk of little else. For me, this kaleidoscope of human color and sound was the wide-open, everyone-belongs America I'd always imagined.

W<small>OOLWORTH'S WAS GOOD</small> to me. It paid the rent, but I needed to save for next year's college fees. So, one day in late June when my shift ended, I headed south to New York Avenue and the Boardwalk, a corner occupied by another iconic shop, McCrory's. McCrory's was a huge company with around 1,300 shops. Legend has it the founder, John Graham McCrorey, dropped the e in his last name to save money on signage, and indeed the shop seemed even more down-market than Woolworth's. McCrory's sold cheap clothes, shoes, cosmetics, jewelry, a small range of food items, and the ubiquitous beach supplies. A soda fountain ran along the right-side wall. A month in Atlantic City had given me the confidence to walk up to the young, fair-haired man behind the counter and ask for a job. He directed me to the store manager.

Chip was from Arizona, transferred to Atlantic City for the summer. He wasn't so much tall as big, a solid mass on the cusp of turning to fat. His thick wedding ring was already sinking into the flesh of his finger. Pointy-toed cowboy boots peeped out from under the hems of his jeans. A turquoise-studded belt kept his plaid, western shirt neatly in place. He seemed old to me, which meant he was probably forty, maybe younger. He slowly looked me up and down. Neither of us liked what we saw, but I needed a second job, and he needed a waitress, so I was hired for the soda fountain, afternoon shift.

McCrory's soda fountain was long. In peak times, it needed at least two waitresses, with the fountain manager, Dave, operating the grill. Dave showed me the ropes: how to replace the huge bladder of milk in the milk dispenser, how to pour pancake batter from the carton stored in the back room into a silver container so customers would think it was made from scratch, how to put a milk shake together with just the right proportion of ice cream. Milk shakes, sundaes, and club sandwiches were all new to me, the commonplace ingredients of my rapidly expanding world, and I was there in the middle of it all in a perky little black apron working a soda fountain. Was there anything more American than a soda fountain? I was the young George Bailey in *It's a Wonderful Life* serving shakes and sundaes in Mr. Gower's drugstore. I felt like a child catching a snowflake on the palm of her hand for the first time.

Wanda, an African American Atlantic City native, worked behind the counter with me. She nodded at me when we were introduced. I could see her take stock, but not in the way Chip had. Approval would be too strong a word for what I saw in her I've-seen-it-all-before eyes, but she didn't disapprove either. We were about the same age. She was a couple of inches taller, with the kind of muscular, strong body I've always wanted. When she smiled, her dark complexion took on a pretty pink undertone. She smiled a lot and advised me to do the same—"You get more tips that way, girl." But the thing I liked most about Wanda was her don't-give-a-shit attitude. She did her job well and followed management's directions without question, but in a detached, wry way, as if she were amused by the endless absurdity of both life and the people who populate it.

In the decades since, I've had close to thirty different jobs, but I have never been so in sync with a colleague as I was with Wanda. We seemed to anticipate each other's moves. If she needed creamer for someone's coffee, I handed it to her without being asked. If I forgot syrup to go with the pancakes I'd just served, she silently left a container of it next to the customer's plate. We moved effortlessly around each other in the tight space behind the counter. We talked too. I told her about my parents and my brothers. I learned that she lived in town with her parents, that she too had brothers. She had a way of skimming over detail, but it didn't matter. I enjoyed her company so much that life outside the present moment seemed unimportant.

Because of Wanda, I looked forward to my afternoons in McCrory's. We laughed a lot, often at things only we found funny. We laughed at Chip's turquoise belt and the way he strutted around in his cowboy boots. We laughed at the way I couldn't grasp the difference between cream cheese and custard Danishes, no matter how hard I tried.

Being left out burned, like failure.

"When are you going to learn, girl?" Wanda asked, pulling two Danishes out of the pastry cabinet on the counter. "This one's cream cheese. This one's custard. Can't you see the difference?" Before that summer, I'd never seen cream cheese, nor a Danish pastry, but somehow, this tip-sucking learning block seemed hilarious.

Having been introduced to American ice cream, I developed a passion that would last a lifetime, matched only by Wanda's love of donuts. We worked out ways we could sneak a bit of both. When she got a customer who wanted ice cream, she let me know. I scooped the ice cream for her customer and sneaked a spoonful for myself. When I got a customer who wanted a donut, I returned the favor—keeping watch as she slid a donut onto a plate for my customer and one into her pocket for nibbling throughout the shift. Our wages were so low, the tips not much better—one customer gave me a religious tract in lieu of a tip "because Jesus is more valuable than gold"—that pangs of conscience about sneaking the odd donut or a spoonful of ice cream were manageable.

Each department of McCrory's had its own manager, mostly students hired for the summer. On my shift that year, the managers seemed as homogenous as Woolworth's liquid eggs—tall, slim, fair-haired, and male. Some evenings, when the tourists who packed the fountain during the afternoon disappeared into restaurants and hotels for dinner, the shop was quiet enough to hear the girls who worked the floor and the managers laughing together. They congregated toward the back of the shop, young, vibrant, unfailingly polite, with straight teeth and clothes that fit just so. They never invited Wanda or me to join them after work.

"You want to be with the pretty white boys, don't you?" Wanda asked one evening as we leaned side by side on the empty counter. She was right. I wanted to be included. Being left out burned, like failure. "Why don't you go talk to them?" she asked. "You're too shy. Go back there and talk to them. Maybe you all will go out tonight."

My mood lifted. "Come with me," I suggested, "we'll both go—" She cut me short with a laugh, then pulled a piece of donut from her apron pocket.

"You want to clean that ice cream fridge? It needs cleaning."

ART AND SPIRITUALITY

S o the summer passed: up early, snatch a quick bowl of cornflakes, head to Woolworth's, shift over, back to the boarding house for a second bowl of cornflakes. Then I'd strap on the black apron, turn right on the Boardwalk, and begin my shift in McCrory's. By August, my waitress uniform was a little loose, and my college fees were in the bank.

Most days were filled with mundane experiences that to me seemed magical—new tastes and smells, new people and places, new friends. The people who thronged the Boardwalk came in all shapes, sizes, and types. Some caught my eye. The elderly white couple shuffled frailly, arm in arm, along the seaward side, dressed as if they were headed to a dinner dance. I fancied they began coming to Atlantic City when the town was still the kind of place where you dressed for dinner. For a couple of days, a beautiful young black woman in a yellow sundress sauntered alone past shops and restaurants, rarely going into any of them. She turned heads, but nobody turned hers. I liked to think of her as serene and self-contained rather than lonely.

One couple, a few years older than me, stood out. They lived in the boarding house across the street. As the bank of cash registers in McCrory's was directly across from the soda fountain, I occasionally spotted them there buying snacks or drinks. The woman was tall and slim, with long, platinum hair that gleamed in the sunshine. Her creamy complexion contrasted starkly with the tanned bodies around her, and somehow the way she held herself—her willowy, pale elegance—made the pursuit of a tan seem crude. Her partner was even taller and as black as she was white. Toned without being over-muscled, he seemed totally at home in his body and carried himself with a dignity that reminded me of Sidney Poitier in every film he ever made. Individually, they were beautiful. Together, they were stunning, like a work of art, a perfectly executed study of light and shade. And for two such beautiful people, they seemed devoid of arrogance or vanity.

One golden afternoon toward the middle of August, the counter in McCrory's was full of customers. A woman—probably in her fifties, maybe sixty—took the last open seat at the edge of my section. I still remember her hair: grey, with a slight curl, pulled back loosely behind her ears. I remember her face, make-up free with high, sculpted cheekbones. After giving her the usual few minutes to peruse the menu, I approached, order pad and pen in hand.

"I'll have coffee and a cheese Danish," she said, and smiled pleasantly.

The coffee was easy. But the Danish! Why did she have to ask for cheese? Why not a fruit I could recognize? I opened the pastry case, my hand hovering between the two options—cheese, custard. I picked one, placed it on a little plate, and put it on the counter beside her coffee. She looked at it, then looked up at me.

"What do you young people think you're trying to prove?" she hissed. Her question seemed bizarre, but it was the manner in which she spoke that rattled me. The venom in her voice was well out of proportion to the sin of serving the wrong Danish, but I couldn't think what else I'd done wrong.

"I'll get you another one," I said, pulling the plate back and thinking I better ask Wanda to double check the replacement pastry. But the woman ignored my fumbling and stared straight at me.

"What do you young people think you're trying to prove?" she repeated and jerked her head backward toward the cash registers. I followed the line of her movement. There at the register, the black and white couple that lived across the street from me were in the process of paying for snacks and what looked like a beach towel.

I stared at the couple for a few seconds, then looked back at my customer. She nodded her head as if to say, "Yeah, now you get it." And I did, in my stomach: a tight, sickening sensation like the world had just turned on its head. Then, a voice in my mind, calm as a college professor explaining an equation, said, "You've heard of racism; well, this is what it looks like." It looked like the triumph on my customer's face when I finally understood that in her America, interracial love

I finally understood that in her America, interracial love was not only taboo, it was abhorrent.

was not only taboo, it was abhorrent. And triumph turned her otherwise pretty features so ugly I could barely look at her. I wrote out her check, slipped it onto the counter, and busied myself with the grill.

For me, *black* and *white* were just words, colors, or, as I learned in science class, not even colors: Black was the absorption and white the reflection of all light, two facets of the same process. But there at the grill in McCrory's, the words I'd always taken at face value sank under the weight of a history uglier than the hatred on my customer's face. It changed forever the way I saw the world. That couple would never again be just two people with movie-star looks who bothered nobody. They were a *black* man and a *white* woman. Wanda would never again be a colleague with whom I shared a sense of humor and an irreverence for authority. She was a *black* colleague. Black. And I was *white*.

A lot of things came clear as I jabbed a scraper at non-existent grease on the already-clean grill. Why, on my first day, the black woman in the window was so angry she yelled at a complete stranger to get out of her neighborhood. Why Wanda's odd remarks about pretty white boys always seemed to conceal the sharp edge of something unsaid. Why she laughed when I suggested we both join the group of staff at the back of the shop. Why the residents of my boarding house were all white, and that black and white couple was the only interracial couple I saw that summer. And I wondered what level of innocence, or naïveté, or stupidity, had shadowed my eyes for the past twenty years.

"You deal with her!" I hissed at the manager when he pointed out that my customer was waiting to pay. He opened his mouth to say something, then did as he was told.

TRAVEL IS AN external act, a sequence of actions leading to a destination that in my case had been predetermined since childhood. But travel is also a journey inward, and it's the journey that, in big or small ways, transforms us. In *Remembrance of Things Past*, Marcel Proust wrote: "The real voyage of discovery consists not in seeking new landscapes, but in seeing with new eyes."[1] That

August, I used some of my savings to buy a thirty-day Greyhound bus ticket and left Atlantic City the same way as had I arrived—on a red, white, and blue bus. As we sped along the New Jersey Turnpike through scenery that, many years in the future, would become the opening sequence of *The Sopranos*, I still had destinations in mind. I thought about where the bus would take me—the wheat fields of Kansas, the Rocky Mountains. Maybe I'd even see the Pacific for the first time. But my journey was already complete. I knew I could never unsee what I'd seen that day in McCrory's, and I wondered what homogenously white Ireland was going to look like when I saw it again with new eyes. •

Catherine Dowling, "With New Eyes," was originally published in Still Points Arts Quarterly 51 (Fall 2023) 28–35. Used with permission of the author.

Disappearing Boy, Scott Avett, 2023, oil on canvas, 61 x 77 in. Used with permission.

Creating Faithfully

By Scott Avett

I STEP INTO THE room. I light the candle and raise the shades. Sunny, the black and orange cat that I found hiding in the sunflower garden last year, rounds the corner and greets me with her five consecutive meows. She sounds particularly dehydrated but very happy to see me. I pause to scratch the top of her head and let her out the door. I look over at my backpack sitting on the printing press. It is overstuffed and heavy. Beside it are a coffee mug, canteen of water, brochure on a neighboring property for sale, my car keys, and two packages from the back porch. I carried all of this through the door, at once, and I think to myself, "Scott, you are doing too much."

ART AND SPIRITUALITY

I am an artist. This building, where Sunny lives, is my studio. I came here today to create, but I don't know how or why. I have interest and ability in many disciplines, therefore there are several rooms in my studio where different forms of creating happen. I especially love painting, though. I love it like I love breathing air. It gives me life. My relationship with it is complex. When I am painting, I can experience moments of ease where I completely forget myself and become lost in the rhythm of the work. Other times, I can find myself deep in process, crippled with doubt and wondering, "What in the world are you doing?" or "What is the use in this? No one is going to get it." Even darker at times, I can tell myself: "This is stupid, you are a hack, and you should quit."

Painting is like living, though. An idea is born, an invitation accepted, and a devotion sustained in a mysterious gift of joy and suffering, from its inception to its end. It is in the deepest and darkest moments of this mystery that I may feel the heaviest of doubts, but I long to create faithfully. To create faithfully, I am asked to follow an idea into darkness, not knowing where it will go or what may come of me. To enter into this mysterious exchange is faith itself. But today I doubt my purpose, and a feeling of despair rushes over me.

A memory of a young boy comes to mind. He steps out of the safety of his lighted room and into the dark unknown of the hallway. It is late at night, and he has heard a noise. He recalls a scary story that he heard his father telling his mother. His world feels unsafe, and there is no telling what will happen to him. He hadn't thought about this before now, but at the age of seven, he has begun to know something different. Up until now, there was no end to the love that he understood. There were no questions about what he was to do or who he

Painting is like living.

was to be. Every moment was eternity, and every distance was infinite. Something is teetering now, and the black abyss between him and the safe arms of his parents shows no mercy. In a way, it shows nothing at all. Now, there are endings to everything he understands, except this dreadful darkness before him. This is awful, and there seems to be no way around it.

Here in the studio, the directions I can go are endless. The ocean of images and sounds is bottomless. The list of tools to make a single mark is infinite. All of this to say one thing, "I am." I have created many forgettable works under different proclamations: "I will," "I want," "I can," "I should," and "I need to" are a few that come to mind. These are the echoes of a world obsessed with "doing it right." I jump in and try my hand at this rightness, but I cease to exist in these moments. I disappear into aspiration and become a stranger to myself and God. In a word, I leave. When I return, however, I arrive in the present. I catch a glimpse of the kingdom of heaven. I am actually invited to do this at every moment, but I slip away again and again. I hide from God, behind my proclamations, until I consent once again, and all these claims fade into the eternal "I am." It is the "I am a child of God" "I am." Everything I do hinges on this very truth.

Another memory of the boy comes to mind. He is in the forest searching for critters: a frog, a crawdad, or even the coveted king snake. As he searches, he finds himself upside down, over the creek, with his arm as far under a rock as he can reach. His entire left arm disappears into the mud. He feels around in the creek sludge for something moving. I have chills thinking about doing this myself. What will bite him? Will his arm get stuck? There is no telling, but he has forgotten about the dangers in the presence of purpose. This eternal thread of purpose is his very lifeline. Nothing matters, not even catching the snake, even though catching the snake is the very activity he is engaged in. He has become, once again, what he has always been: a child of God. The boy dissolves into the leaf-covered mossy creek bed and becomes one with the forest. Somehow, he is more real the more he disappears.

The woods that he becomes part of are the same woods that I ran in as a child. My father bought this acreage with money that he earned as a welder back in the 1980s. I own the deed to this land now. How I make a living pays for the taxes on this property. Am I working today for that reason—to make a living? Do I need to be productive in this moment to secure the well-being of my family and our possessions? Sounds like critical work. A choice that matters. I want to be lost in my work, like the boy, but it's impossible to forget myself when making a living feels urgent. I decide to protest by sitting in my chair and praying.

I am instantly distracted with the urge to get busy. Thoughts bounce back and forth, and I feel a sense of shame and inadequacy. I am here to work, but I am completely distracted by my habitual neurotic tendencies. I start obsessing about some wrong that has been done. I feel a particular disdain for the systems in which I operate: the schools, corporations, churches, neighborhoods, and families. These systems all contain hypocrisy, like me, but I look to identify them as challengers. I think of them as the culprits in my stagnation. The presence of this idea intensifies the questions. Why are you doing this? How are you to do this? Where does this fit in? In the balance of creating faithfully and making a living, perhaps the question was never, "Why am I doing this?" but, instead, "For whom am I doing this?"

I think of Jesus Christ: how he spoke, what he said, and how he lived in this broken world with a body that would be broken and destroyed too. I contemplate Jesus' identity. I consider how he knew exactly who he was. I think that this truth, alone, separates him from us. I can see how this knowing of who one is can be the most loving truth one can offer. I consider what this means to me. Jesus' life shows me who to be when I have lost direction, a way to do an impossible thing. This unconditional love provides me with eternal companionship. The realization that one is never alone is the seed from which true freedom grows.

I often try to avoid solitude. I work, I play, I prepare, I clean, I talk, I dine, I shop, I exercise, and so on. It is true that all these things are necessary, but when the dust has settled from all my hyperactivity, I am faced once again with solitude. This time alone is the fertile ground where I cultivate my purpose. My contribution is my engagement in it. This studio is my cloister. To pray is to be drawn nearer to my existence. The only control I have is to show up and respond. I build from this simple idea.

I am alone today, but what good is solitude without purpose? I long for more direction, but the indicators from outside myself are weighed down with expectations. These expectations have no place here. My purpose is to create, but I can't force it into place. I aim for truth, but my own awareness of it destroys its purity. I long to create faithfully, rather than successfully, productively, intelligently, or even truthfully. Creating faithfully is not knowing how to do it. It is believing that it is worth doing. This leaves me looking to forget myself and to unlearn all the rules and realities that swirl around in my mind. I long to dissolve into my work like the boy in the forest. The only remedy in this moment is to act, but on what?

And so I fall in aspiration, and I rise back up in humility. The truth is mysterious, but always there. God ushers me closer to it. With this, I accept everything. This includes unchangeable suffering as well as the responsibility to address unjust and healable suffering. In the end, I simply hope to be obedient to who I am, a child of God, and not what I do, a "contender of men." With this, I replace the anxiety-ridden aspirations of arrival with peace in a true being. This is who I am in Christ and who Christ is in me. I will contend among people, but I will do it knowing that it is temporal. What a precious revelation. Simply put, to create faithfully is to be me.

Ideas gather and call out to me. I greet each one, being as childlike as possible. I accept this liberating sonship. I empty my heart and my mind, and I gaze. I can see all the terrible beauty that surrounds me. The smell of the forest, where life and death make way for each other constantly. The Sun that traces bright shapes on the paint-splattered wood floor, warmth for the cat to bask in. The same shapes that were painted pale blue by the silent moon at the wretched hour of the wolves. I see the mysterious fog and crystal beads of dew at morning's return. The gnarly eastern cedar with the funny baritone voice. The sincerity in the sheep's eyes. The oily black rooster named Pikachu, limping across the farmyard. Marek's Disease will take his life within a week. He, with his single purpose: to eat and drink.

I see and hear all these creations, ever-changing, ever proclaiming the glory of God. This is love, not happiness. This is joy, not health. This is truth, not history. I ask myself, "What do I do?" and I answer with the only thing I know. "Act like God. Trust that you are being you. Trust that truth and love are inseparable. Trust that this single moment is that very truth."

My words fail to describe it, and I am riddled with brokenness. "How do I love you?" I ask. All I can do is listen. I long to accept the next invitation. The glow of a white panel faces me. Now I know where these hours are to be spent. This was all that I was asking. Every other question was answered when I was asked, "Are you willing to accept that who you are is, and always has been, enough?" And I answered . . . "I am." •

When Body Speaks:
On Dance as Spiritual Practice

By Jenna Keiper

The body says what words cannot.
—Martha Graham

Mystery upon mystery.
—Bonnie Badenoch

D ANCE IS MY first language. It was the first way I knew myself, and it was the first way I connected to God, or Spirit, or Divine. Before ascension-obsessed theology and sex-phobic subculture got ahold of me to declare Body *so terribly distracting and profane*, my six-year-old Body danced freely in the woods outside our country home.

Body listened to the way the leaves explained mysteries to my leaping, glowing, ecstatic heart. Body heard wisdom in the wind and unknowable knowings in the smell of pine needles and dogwood flowers. Body, all gangly legs and dirty elbows, responded by spinning and flowing along with the creek and the clouds.

My confession: I struggle to contain Body inside what is widely considered "contemplative prayer," or "meditation," or the more systematic realms of Spirit. I struggle to make headway in traditional "talk therapy" because intellect-obsessed and Mind-only systems keep many concepts from diving deeper, only skimming the surface of my understanding. They never seem to make their way into any lasting kind of change.

My pathway to "mindfulness" or "contemplation" or "trance" or "Divine" is, and always has been, through movement. The deepest understandings and inner shifts only come for me when Mind and Spirit are intricately connected to, and in harmony with, my Body. And so, as this is my first language and the first and primary way I connect with the Sacred, I extend the invitation to you, fellow travelers: Come dance with me.

T HE FLYER ON the door says 5 Rhythms.[1] I hike up two stories into an open space with wood floors and wide windows that open to the sky. I drop bag onto bench, shoes onto floor, and smile shyly at the woman with the graying hair. Wrapping Body tightly in a blanket to start because life is so confusing—*I feel so vulnerable. Am I going to be okay?*—I step onto the floor.

Threading my way through other arriving Bodies—the sitting ones, the spinning ones, the slowly limbering ones—I find a free spot on the outskirts. Sitting, I nod at the guide behind her computer at the front. She smiles in return, her playlist's rhythm bringing us in, warming us up. Hiding in my blanket, I melt forward, face on the floor, breathe.

Oneing

Hello Body.
It's me. It's you. It's we.

Last month, my partner and I officially broke the home we built with so much hope and sweetness. This morning found me on hands and knees, dry-heaving grief onto the kitchen floor. Alone, my Body postures a backward birth. Up through my throat, Body ejects the poison of this weight from my diaphragm. When there is a metaphorical death, maybe it comes up through the throat as bile rather than being birthed through the root.

I cleaned my face and came here after.

Hello, my love. Here I am.

I find the glowing internal place that blossoms at the light, attentive touch.

Here I am.

This quiet blossoming holds all the trembling parts of me. *Hello, my love.* Music rises. Our guide opens space with prompts for inner wanderings and outer exploration. Eyes closed, I am attentive to my Body in relation to the other Bodies around me and begin to listen... deep... within this swirling tenderness. We start our journey, connecting to our inmost selves and holding the company of each other with sacredness and grace.

I. **Flowing,** *first rhythm*

circles
i am circles and curving
    the space around me fluid, a partnered dance with
        space and time, limbs caressing the air
            body spills through the molecules of
                oxygen and argon
                gentle in its sensual
            earthy play following the velvet grooves of gravity
            and bone, the
        hand of time slides slowly up my spine. I follow vertebrae by
    vertebrae, skin stretch and hips roll into this sacred embrace
        steady always moving
        the dripping honey texture of the molecules of me
                                    Surrender.

I SLOWLY COME HOME to myself, to Spirit.² (*ah, Divine!*) Listening, listening, responding. This is a "way of attending,"³ a way of paying attention that centers the wordless knowledge beyond the inflexible crust and vigilance of my left-centered brain and culture. It is a conscious surrender to the "flowing relational world"⁴ without attempting to parse, to dissect, to define. It is a surrender of conscious understanding to a wisdom far more ancient than our cultural obsession with Enlightenment. *I let go, I let through, I surrender.*

Body warms, blanket shed, I'm not alone. My solo journey is happening together in a community of journeys. Some wild in the center of the floor, others small and fragile on the outskirts, we're all holding space together as we each connect to the sensation of being in Bodies. In-bodied. *Embodied*. Of re-membering the muscle and bone. Of being with the pain in the tissues of the ankle and the hip. From this remembering, we move to the sensations that clench the solar plexus, the electricity that shoots down the spine, the heat that rises in the neck, the face.⁵ We have named these things:

Fear.

Excitement.

Anger.

We regain our curiosity and step back from our attachment to or refusal of these processes that move across our systems.⁶ *Welcome, welcome.* We hold space for them:

Unsticking.

Unblocking.

Allowing them to ripple and move through by literally moving through. Growing our capacity for clean pain.⁷

Thank you Mind for caring for me
in the way you know how.
It's safe to rest now.

It's time for Body to bring forward what is underneath. I bring consciousness back to the inmost place. Swaying gently. Breathing in, breathing out. *I'm listening, love.* Something opens deep inside me. Something... pushed down, an attempted annihilation of exiled parts. It pulses. It breaks. What is this massive rush bubbling to the surface? I feel it, rhythm changes—

II. **Staccato**, *second rhythm*

BURST of heat across my chest
and through to the ends of my
fingers, follow the electric impulses
of edges, of enough, of CRUSHING
and BREAKING through and intensity
of my weight pendulum

> HIT.
> Pushing up to slam the earth with
> being, HERE I am not annihilated.
> You do not get to CRUSH me here. I
> AM. Break the shell the veneer the
> glass the chain, this is my elbow you feel
> it take my taut energy funnel it,
> the scorched fire earth of it, combine
> the elements, electricity through my
> clenched fingers my
>
> PUNCH

my mouth intensity BOILS
let it through let it through
let it through this
is also sacred.

Power.

I SURRENDER TO THIS movement in my little corner of the room. My inmost Self in collaboration with Body guides my shapes and movements as I complete the actions[8] I was once powerless to take. Healing. My systems relax as I wordlessly enact a boundary, communicate existence, and move through physical space the words I was once unable to speak.

Many of us have lost connection to our own knowing and our own voices, to the knowledge of a true Sacred Yes and a true Sacred No, to the ability to listen and move with that stillest, smallest Voice. (*ah, Divine!*) Many of us were taught by religion or culture to deeply mistrust our inside Selves. "Your heart is deceitful," they said. Some

ART AND SPIRITUALITY

of us numb, and ignore, and justify away the clenching and trembling *something is wrong please do something, change something.* I didn't listen then, but I'm listening now.

In every moment of human existence, our brain structures register background feelings and information.[9] Vastly more information stays hidden in our implicit knowing than ever surfaces into our conscious brains. This is our "wordless knowledge,"[10] and today, in this dancing space, I provide a space for it to speak. *Let through, let through.*

The music shifts, and as we enter the third rhythm, a resistance hardens inside me. I am, as is common at this point, ramping up into visceral terror. This is the most difficult rhythm for me, as it requires a profound surrender. I attend my resistance. I broker a willingness to release control. Rhythmically, jaw unclenched, arms unhindered, I release. *Here I am. I'm willing. Teach me.*

III. Chaos, *third rhythm*

\And everything fractures\

CRushed glasS and frayed eD ges.
        Color (and light) and
                awkwar d   limbs
                     that *clank*
     are (not) beaUtiful and judge
                  ments   *clatter*
             and   letting [Go.]
      Wind whiPs the sand tornadoes a bird flies
      beneath the ocean—
      the edges of me d I s s o l v
                    e
and my hand is> (not) with my *arm* is not with my stoMach is> (not) with my foot is with myelbowiswithmy back is with my *hair* that DraPes across m y facEas I vomit the
        BILE OF ALL THE PRETTY Concept {s]
      where is the ground
and expectations that poi2on my insi des
     they are nO t mine to   hold
   +anymore;

       Release.

And oh, how we fear the unknown. My dominance-obsessed culture does not prepare me well to withstand, let alone thrive, in this inevitable human rhythm of chaos and fog. We must learn it. We must practice, through meditation, through tears, through dance.

This movement follows the energies and deep, deep calm (*ah Divine!*) that reside at my center, connecting and reconnecting and connecting again to the inmost Self. Ah, the pain and pressure of it. Ah, the discomfort of this repatterning, this listening depth. Unfamiliar. So, I practice. I follow Body's wisdom.

A white lance of charged pain (some might call it wailing grief) flashes across my chest and into my belly. There is a weight that pulls me down from the lowest ribs, and all the strength bleeds out of my muscles, and I am on the floor: Roadkill.

The other dancers move around me. Their bodies find their own rhythms and twists and expansions and contractions and shakes and smoothness, and they are with me, but they are not invasive of me. We are doing this together, and now I am the carrion left on the local highway after life was going twenty over the speed limit and didn't stop when I so innocently stepped out into the road.

The wisps of memories and voices, terrified and sobbing, flit and echo between my cells. A face. A holding that is no longer here. This grief! *Welcome, welcome.* I hold space for this intensity. *I'm here, my love.* The other dancers fill the space with their holding. They too are riding the waves of their lives. I am not alone.

And I am carrion. Crushed, completely, by the bitter waves of a battered heart. Not dead, just flattened, breathing in the sweetness of a wise wood floor and feeling safe to be here, just as I am, and nobody looks at me strangely, and this life-flattening is welcome here too. I don't have to pretend.

I could stay here for the rest of the session—but I don't. I stay as long as Body brings me rest, and she keeps me there for a little while—maybe five minutes, maybe twenty. But soon a song plays electricity, and Body whispers for me to wiggle my fingers and my toes and then to slowly stand and then to sway, and then I'm up and off again, joining in the fray.

IV. Lyrical, *fourth rhythm*

>   Up.
>   A soft glow breathes,
>   warm air lifts the balloon of me effortlessly.
>   Head floating, feet learning the textures of new earth, heart
>   opens to the sky. Bounce in time with friendly knees, cross the wide
>   space. Potential emerges behind my sternum circles me lubricated
>   joints find specific flat of hand creates structures in the negative space
>   light heart leaps to find balance tarsals
>   take up their shape to hold the magnificent
>   electric continents of me all parts gentle
>   harmony so that together we bend
>   and stretch and align and plant and love
>   and grow and laugh and grow.   *Create.*

THERE IS JOY here too. I am curious as I touch it, so fully inhabiting my Body that it comes to me as the way I lift my heart space to the sky, head falling back, eyes closed. Not a concept—a way of being. *Here I am.* Joy and grief and pain and anger and love and healing, together.

We connect to Self so we can be in right alignment with that still, small knowing deep within. (*ah, Divine!*) We seek right alignment so we can relate and connect to other humans with both balance and generosity. We relate and connect to other humans so we can build together, heal together, create the wild and beautiful neighborhoods in which each human moves comfortably in their own shape and values the unique shapes of others.

My ancestors, the wild siblings of old oak forests and the ruddy wanderers of windy peaks, knew communal rhythmic movement. All our ancestral indigenous communities—as far as we can possibly know—have danced in community rituals to cope with the terror and awe of human life.[11] Anthropologists the world over have found the practice of communal dance to be fascinating in its predictability. It's so very…human. Humans have, all along, had the answers today's scientists "discover" written in our communal rhythms. Perhaps it would be wise to listen.

Remember, electrons whisper as the music slows, *remember*. Together, our Bodies calm and soften. Many Bodies lead their Souls into positions on the floor. Curling and rocking, our breathing slows, together. *Remember*.

V. Stillness, *final rhythm*

Worlds exist in my shoulder and unfold, piece
by integrating piece, through elbow, wrist, metacarpus,
   knuckle, fingerprint.   Every atom of me I feel in
tandem with atoms that are not me and
we melt, together.   A slow fire
inside connects to the ground that holds me;
weight on my hands, weight on my knees, cradling
   me, gently.   The earth, Mother, welcomes my slowness,
my all and my everything, my nothing.   I am nothing. I am
   everything.   Time drips, electrons fall into the
earth, I disintegrate once again into carbon and feed the seeds so
   they can grow.   In their
   time.
I am nothing, and I hold the universe.

   Whole.

UNWORDED KNOWINGS, KNOWN. Embodied unknowings, unknown. I ride this ecstatic wave in strength and safety back down into linear time, my spine supported by the nurturing earth. I invite the balance of Body-Mind-Spirit to reintegrate, to come back into their braided co-creation, to work together in harmony as I navigate a human life. Body ushered into her sacred and rightful place, alongside Mind and Spirit. All three functioning best when connected and balanced by the others: my personal trinity. (*ah, Divine!*)

   I am raw, but I am whole. Emptied, but full. A healing work birthed today through the kinesthetic patterns of radical surrender, loving boundaries, necessary destruction, creative connection, and caring reconstruction. Holding opposites together and learning, through

Body, how to live between them, among them, through them. Honoring all rhythms[12] with their necessary wisdoms.

God in the earth. God in the trees. God in myself. God, embodied. She speaks through every Body, and so the invitation is extended to every Body: Gray hair, unlined faces, stiff joints, supple muscles. Tall and short and bigger-bodied. Slow, quick, pregnant, dying. Alone in your room or on the floor in community. If you have a Body that moves in any way, then movement is your birthright. And if your Body can no longer move, then we will find a way to move in energy with you. Welcome, fellow travelers. Where words fade, the Body speaks.

Mystery upon mystery.

My Conscious Movement Lineage:
I am deeply grateful to my therapist, Jess, for leading me to a solo 5 Rhythms practice, to Chloe Goodwin (5 Rhythms) and Jenny Macke (Open Floor) for guiding me in communal practice, and to Jillian Froebe for witnessing me in Authentic Movement, a form of expressive movement therapy.

Meeting a Creative God in the Arts

By Mark Longhurst

O NE OF THE rather glorious benefits of living in Western Massachusetts, as I do, is the art. Come summer, the rural and relatively quiet towns near me are bustling with people. They're here for the Williamstown Theater Festival, a well-respected summer theater program that holds sway with the New York City crowd. They're here for MASS MocA, one of the largest contemporary art museums in the country, also known for rousing bluegrass, rock, and experimental music festivals. They're here for Tanglewood, the Boston Symphony Orchestra's summer home. And it's not only the New York and Boston wealthy who soak up the fun, either. Locals like me usher for free theater, picnic at free outdoor concerts, and meet up with friends at the festivals.

It only made sense, then, to combine summer worship at church with summer art. When I pastored a church in Williamstown, Massachusetts, I sought to counteract a characteristic summer attendance slump by engaging during worship with what everyone engaged in the rest of their lives: the summer art scene. Each Sunday, we curated the prayers, Scripture passages, sermons, and occasional post-church discussions around the exhibitions and performances. This experiment, which I called Art and Soul, resulted in Sunday prayers quoting playwright William Inge (1913–1973), a series on the nineteenth-century Dutch Post-Impressionist painter Van Gogh's struggle with Christianity, visionary photographs about environmental catastrophe from Senegal-based artist Fabrice Monteiro, and more. And it worked. Instead of people "taking off church" in the summer, we created an energizing conversation and connected with our community.

The more I have married my appreciation for art with my dedication to prayer and the study of Scripture, the more creative my spiritual life has become. Prayer is now like art—as Matthew Fox describes, "a radical response to life."[1] And God, for me, is no longer the dissatisfied dictator of my childhood—God *is* creativity itself, and the arts express God's passion for life.

After all, in the beginning, God *created* (Genesis 1:1). And whether birthing the universe, forming a people, or liberating the enslaved, much of what God does in the Bible is *creative*. There's something intrinsic to God that pulses with new possibility, which is to say that there's something inherently creative in the nature of whatever we mean when we talk about God.

IN THE HEBREW imagination, God's first creative act takes place through speech. God in Genesis 1 is a spoken-word poet constructing worlds. God says, "Let there be light," and there is light (Genesis 1:3). In Genesis 2, God crosses artistic genres, trying out sculpting and gardening too. God makes the heavens and the earth and shapes the first human from the dust. God breathes into the human's nostrils the breath of life, plants a garden in Eden, and makes fruitful trees grow.

As the Bible's story continues, God's creative experiments develop and echo through its pages. After creating a cosmos in Genesis, God creates a people in the book of Exodus. God separates water from dry land at the Red Sea, allowing the Israelite people to flee their Egyptian enslavers, echoing the first creation (Exodus 14–15). John's gospel understands Christ—who also goes by "the Word"—as inherently creative: "In the beginning was the Word, and the Word was

God is creativity itself, and the arts express God's passion for life.

with God, and the Word was God; through him all things were made" (John 1:1). Christ the Word is present at creation, participating in the art-making that formed our world.

God is creative, Christ is creative, and the universe that God creates is creative. The Big Bang explodes, and new possibilities expand. Something that does not exist begins to exist. Astronomer Adam Frank describes that original creative moment of the universe: "In the beginning, there was a single geometrical point containing all space, time, matter, and energy. This point did not sit in space. It was space. There was no inside and no outside. Then 'it' happened. The point exploded and the universe began to expand."[2] God and the universe are inherently creative, and perhaps that's because God and the universe are related. They are not separate.

If God is creative and the universe God created is creative, we might expect the religion that follows this creative God to flourish in its relationship with creativity, especially through the arts. On the one hand, Christianity and the cultures it has inhabited have contributed mightily to the creative arts. Medieval painting traditions famously featured biblical scenes such as Moses and the Ten Commandments, David and Goliath, Mary's Annunciation, the Nativity, or Jesus' Last Supper.

It's also worth noting that the Bible *is* art. The sixty-six books that Protestants like me call the Bible are a massive library containing every genre one could imagine: poetry, tall tales, wisdom sayings, eroticism, science fiction, and fantasy. On the other hand, sometimes the Hebrew Bible and New Testament carry a deep antagonism toward "the other," including the sacred art, cultures, and religions of non-Israelite peoples. "You must not make a carved image for yourself," God tells Moses and the ancient Israelites (Exodus 20:4), leveling a damning critique of Egyptian sacred objects.

The religious history of Christianity unfolds with a paradox of both embracing and rejecting the arts. Sacred art and images used within the Christian faith become caught up in this tension. Take, for example, Eastern Orthodox Christians and Protestant Christians. Eastern Orthodox have believed for centuries that images or icons reveal the presence of God. They point out that Jesus is the "image" or icon of the invisible God (Colossians 1:15). As part of their worship, they include painted pictures of Jesus, stories from the gospels, and saints of the church.

On the other hand, Protestants became infamous for their passionate opposition to images in church. Perhaps the most dramatic example of this opposition is a radical strain of Lutherans who became iconoclastic—which, translated from the Greek, means "image destroyer." These image-destroying Protestants shattered stained-glass windows and tore down church paintings. They even fomented riots, such as one in Basel, Switzerland that resulted in throwing art into fire, tearing down statues, and painting over frescoes.[3]

Christianity is conflicted about the arts, and never more so than through the false religious dichotomy of the sacred and the secular. Everyday mystics who understand that heaven and earth are entwined do not recognize such a split. For such seers, like the angels in the prophet Isaiah's vision, there is one sacred reality, and "the whole earth is full of God's glory" (Isaiah 6:3). Yet Christian history is full of those who chose fearful rejection of this world over the joyful mystery of incarnation. For such people, there is sacred art that deals with Christian themes like paintings of the Madonna and Child, the music of George Frideric Handel (1685–1759) or, say, contemporary Christian musicians like Michael W. Smith. Then there's the secular

> All life is sacred, and to call a part of reality "secular" is simply a failure to appreciate reality.

world, where everything else resides—but the dividing line between sacred and secular leads to fundamentalism.

THE THEOLOGY OF incarnation gives me hope that modern Christians might make pathways toward unabashedly celebrating the creative arts. Incarnational theology tries to make sense of a mystery by asking what it might mean that Jesus the Son of God is also the Son of Humanity. The early theologians said that he is somehow both: divine *and* human at the same time. But the incarnation of Jesus also unleashes the incarnation of reality: If the creative God has incarnated the divine self in human, material life through Jesus, then human and material life are divine. And if human and material life are inherently divine, then there is no separation between sacred and secular. All life is sacred, and to call a part of reality "secular" is simply a failure to appreciate reality.

Honoring one sacred reality gives us freedom to recognize and receive God in the arts, and not only Christian art or classical art, either. God is revealed through all of reality just as Jesus incarnated and experienced the full range of human experience. This means that God is not only present in stereotypically beautiful or pretty things, but also in tragedy and pain—or maybe God's beauty is different from our own and itself *contains* the tragic, absurd, and agonizing. As theologian Karl Barth (1886–1968) wrote, "God's beauty embraces death as well as life, fear as well as joy, what we might call ugly as well as what we might call the beautiful."[4] The arts are an invitation to encounter God's creative presence in reality, which is to say that we find God in the holy ordinary. We meet God in the arts, yes, and also in the death, life, fear, joy, ugliness, and beauty of our own lives and world. •

This excerpt from The Holy Ordinary: Everyday Mysticism for Troubled Times, *by Mark Longhurst, is used by permission of Monkfish Book Publishing, Rhinebeck, NY and is to be published in October 2024.*

Santo Domingo Pueblo pottery, Robert Tenorio, approximately 30 years old, 32 x 13 in., Santa Maria de la Vid Abbey, NM. Used with permission.

The Abbey as Art Repository

By Joel Garner

ART AND SPIRITUALITY

For centuries, abbeys and monasteries have been places where good art has been acquired, appreciated, and safely kept. While art commission and acquisition were not primary goals for Norbertine communities, they have certainly been of importance in terms of what we do.

I N NEW MEXICO, we had an opportunity to build the youngest abbey church within our 900-year-old tradition. The Norbertine presence in Albuquerque began when five of us were missioned to come to New Mexico from St. Norbert Abbey in Wisconsin in 1985 to found an abbey.

Part of the Norbertine charism has been to meet the needs of the local church as we find them. In other words, we don't have a particular ministry focus. For example, when we came to Wisconsin in the latter part of the nineteenth century, we encountered so many immigrants who wanted to be educated. They felt basically that the US was Protestant. As a result, we founded several Catholic schools.

Preparing to move to New Mexico, we talked about what we wanted to accomplish when we came. One aspect in the forefront of our conversations was that we knew it was a different culture from the Midwest. We wanted to be as sensitive as we could to this new culture, what it might say to us, and how we might respond in a positive fashion. That has been a backdrop for us since we arrived.

We initially purchased thirty acres, south of Albuquerque, which had been owned by the Archdiocese of Santa Fe. We had this dream of constructing a beautiful little abbey. The archdiocese then offered to sell us the adjacent forty acres and six buildings, which had been a Dominican Retreat House for some years.

Initially, we did not think it was a good idea. But, as we talked about it over an entire year in our monthly community days, the idea shifted from "We shouldn't do this" to "Maybe we should," then to "Yes, we should," then finally to "It's the best decision we've ever made." Those six buildings provided the infrastructure that advanced us more quickly toward becoming an abbey.

O UR ABBEY CHURCH is Santa Maria de la Vid, Our Lady of the Vine. We chose that name because of the Hispanic influence in this area, as well as making an historical connection with one of the first Norbertine abbeys, constructed in Spain in the twelfth century.

The Blessed Sacrament Chapel has this big window which frames the Rio Grande Valley, surrounding woodland bosque, and the Sandia Mountains. So, we see the Cosmic Christ there in addition to the Sacrament of Christ.

All the woodwork in the Abbey Church was done by a local woodworker, Chris Sandoval, of Artisans in the Desert. The striking maple Tabernacle is fronted with a cloisonné image of Jesus' hands breaking bread over a broken world, created by the Norbertine artist Fr. Stephen Rossey.

The pavers and colors in the church reflect both the culture and something of the solidity of our tradition. The block walls—you sense they are going to be there forever. The circle inlaid in the floor represents the Native American kiva, the inner prayer space set aside within the broader community.

The colors in the windows are the Native American colors for the directions. The arches in the church are not structural. They are meant to create more of an intimate space here, and the cloth baffles filter the direct desert sunlight.

The Abbey Church contains pottery from different pueblos that was gifted to us by friends at the Palms Trading Company. There is also a 1910 Navajo chieftain's blanket that was donated by a local family. The eldest adult child said, "We're not going to fight over this anymore. We're giving it to you."

As we sought to find local artists with whom to collaborate, we made a good friend who was head of the municipal program which allocates 1 percent of general obligation bonds and certain revenue bonds for the purchase or commission of works of art. He was in touch with a lot of artists and so helped us make some important connections.

Usually, in a Norbertine refectory or dining room, there is a depiction of the Last Supper. In 2020, we decided to commission a triptych. Three local artists were invited to submit preliminary sketches, and we chose Nicholas Otero from nearby Los Lunas, New Mexico. Apprenticed to master artists at age sixteen, Otero has gained a significant reputation for his work with traditional methods, natural pigments, and hand-carved panels.

For our triptych of meal scenes from scripture, on the left is the wedding feast at Cana of Galilee (John 2:1–11). On the right is Jesus multiplying the loaves and fishes (Matthew 14:13–21). The center panel depicts the washing of the feet at the Last Supper (John 13:2–17) instead of the usual table filled with disciples. At the top, you see the Holy Spirit diving down.

There is a great story about the original owner of the building that houses our refectory. He was a World War II fighter pilot who had a Piper Cub and a music store on historic Route 66 in Albuquerque. After the war, he delivered musical instruments to kids around the state. He was coming back from El Paso and made an emergency landing on Old Coors Road. He walked up the hill to find help and said, "Oh my God, look at this view!" For the next three years, he badgered the ranchers who owned the place to sell him the property. Eventually, they did. He bought seventy acres in 1947. Ten years later, he was going through a divorce and had to sell the house. Dominican Sisters from Philadelphia bought it and built the first retreat center in the Archdiocese of Santa Fe on the property.

In recent years, four different spiritual retreat centers in this area have closed for a variety of reasons. In effect, we are the only one left. So, our particular ministry focus is clear: The need is for a place where people can come to renew and refresh their spiritual life. Therefore, we launched a capital campaign to expand our facilities. We constructed four new hermitages in a beautiful setting and then added twenty-eight beds to our existing facilities, enabling us to welcome more than fifty people for overnight stays.

Naturally, we needed a larger space in which to gather. So, we expanded Our Lady of Guadalupe Commons with a classroom and a larger conference room that seats over 200. For this facility, we commissioned a *bulto* or sculpture of Nuestra Señora de Guadalupe by the great New Mexican *santero* Felix Lopez.

Felix Lopez carved a unique *bulto* from local woods that fits with our southwestern setting. In his words,

> The image of Our Lady of Guadalupe I carved in bass wood. The crown is aspen; the crescent moon and base are ponderosa pine, and the backing with the rays of the sun is also pine. The altar is sugar pine and designed and carved in the Spanish colonial style. There is not a single nail in either the bulto or the altar.
>
> For more than three decades, I have been making my own water-based pigments from local minerals, clays and plants, as was done by the santeros in colonial times when there were no art supply stores. I have done a lot of experimentation with colors I extract from nature. . . . Before painting the bulto, it is necessary to coat it with two or three applications of pulverized gypsum (gesso) which acts as a primer. I also make my own gesso. As a binder in applying the color, I use the yolk of the egg, or rabbit skin glue, so the pigment adheres to the gesso.[1]

THE ABBEY IS also fortunate to have a collection of pottery from Native American Pueblos in New Mexico. Here is the story. The Rev. Richard Ver Bust was a priest in the Green Bay Diocese who had a doctorate in historical theology from Marquette University and taught at St. Norbert College in Wisconsin.

He first came to our abbey to help establish a satellite location for the Master of Theological Studies program of St. Norbert College.

When he retired, he would spend the semester here to teach a course and enjoy the desert environment. It was an ecumenical venture from the beginning, because we entered into a partnership with the New Mexico Conference of Churches.

As part of the process of accrediting the master's program, we had to demonstrate that we had a library worthy of a graduate program. That is why we put some energy into the library.

At one point, early on in that process, I was up at St. Norbert College, where I had been on the board of trustees for many years. I was in the art gallery, saw a group of Native American pots on display, and realized, "My God, these are New Mexican pots!" It turned out that they were from Fr. Ver Bust's collection. I had no idea he had collected so much pottery when he would visit and teach.

The next time he came to teach, he sat down with me and said, "Joel, I know you want a library. What I'd like to do is this. I'll give you my pots and you can sell them and fund the library."

After he died, I went to his house, and there were boxes and boxes with pots in them. Over the years, he had collected 360 pots. Talk about God's Providence!

The next issue was, like with gemstones or diamonds, how do you know what they are worth? We had a woman in the master's program who, along with her husband, owned a gallery in downtown Albuquerque. So, we approached them to see if they would be interested in buying them. All we wanted to keep was one pot from each pueblo.

The collection was valued at $200,000, which made a huge difference in funding the library. We kept just seventeen pieces, one from each pueblo that makes pottery. Those are now displayed in the entrance hallway to the bright and well-stocked library.

I SHAKE MYSELF SOMETIMES because we are in the midst of a lot of natural beauty here. I get up every morning, and I see the sun rising from across the valley, and I say, "How did I ever get here?" People come here and say, "Oh my God, look at this!"

We want to be careful not to lose that sense in any way, but rather to enhance what is here naturally. It also impacts the way we have built our buildings and the care we have taken. We have used the same architect and construction company for everything from the beginning, working from a cohesive overall design.

In all our public spaces there is some art that speaks to an aspect of the Catholic tradition, which has always respected the artist and art. For most of our time here, we have been spending to build buildings rather than commission art. But we did commission the bronze artwork in the Abbey Church, the meal triptych in the dining room, and the Nuestra Señora de Guadalupe. These exquisite images are meant to create or contribute to a prayerful atmosphere.

When I first arrived in New Mexico, the southwestern artwork contained topics and images I wasn't engaged with right away. But as I began to understand where they came from, who made them, and what they expressed, I personally came to a greater appreciation of the art.

Clearly, art makes a contribution to what we are about here: providing an opportunity for people to come to a place which has a natural beauty and a spiritual sense to it. People will say, "Gosh, I just arrived, and already I feel different." •

1 : Henri Matisse, Chapelle du Rosaire, Vence, France, altar with window and figure of St. Dominic, 1947–1951. Hackenberg-Photo-Cologne / Alamy Stock Photo.

The Persistent Resurgence of Sacred Architecture

By Karla Cavarra Britton

ART AND SPIRITUALITY
101

Every so often there is a compelling need for sacred space even within everyday life, an incontrovertible necessity that has been confirmed over the centuries by sublime examples, and that has now re-emerged decisively, perhaps in an extreme attempt to respond to the incompleteness of the contemporary dimension.

—Mario Botta[1]

SACRED ARCHITECTURE HAS consistently played a significant role as an arena for experimentation and innovation by many prominent architects. As the Portuguese architect Álvaro Siza has noted, it is possible "to do the history of architecture, through the history of religious buildings."[2]

Throughout the twentieth and twenty-first centuries, a remarkable outpouring of new sacred works has challenged the very idea of what a religious building is and what role it plays in its social and cultural contexts.[3] (This resurgence is evident across religious traditions, but this short article will remain focused on its Christian manifestation.) Such an effusion in the Western-European context is the result of what Jürgen Habermas noted is religion's reassertion in the shaping of social and political life, defying the so-called secularization hypothesis which held that growing modernization would necessarily result in increased secularism.[4]

In contemporary pluralist societies, the consensus of spiritual and cultural meaning has disappeared, and with it the coherent symbolic patterns from which an architect could draw to endow a building with a sense of the sacred. In this regard, architects today are often placed in a vulnerable position by asserting their own understanding of the concept of the sacred. As Rafael Moneo, who in 2002 designed the Cathedral of Our Lady of the Angels in Los Angeles, observed, the result is that an architect must now "take a risk" in designing sacred space, asserting their own interpretation or vision of what constitutes religious experience.[5]

The concern for reimagining spiritual meaning in built form takes on particular urgency in a radically fissiparous social environment where technological and economic forces assert their overwhelming dominance. The built spaces and urban landscapes in which we live often exhibit an overwhelmingly dehumanizing prevalence. The proliferation of the resulting "junk space" suggests that ours is a world that we have built but which we do not—at least subconsciously—wish to inhabit. To take the risk of inserting into such a configuration a building that speaks of more transcendent values is therefore not only countercultural, but, in many ways, counterintuitive as well. Or, as Moneo argues, it is a risk.

A frequently invoked trope for architects designing contemporary sacred works is the nonfigurative ideal of the ineffable, originally championed by the Franco-Swiss architect Le Corbusier (1887–1965). In particular, his designs for the pilgrimage chapel of Notre-Dame du Haut (1950–1955) in northeastern France and the Dominican monastery of Sainte Marie de La Tourette (1952–1960) near Lyon continue to serve as points of inspiration. These buildings exemplify Le Corbusier's fascination with the possibility of opening up a fourth dimension—which is how he understood the "ineffable"—when there is a precise alignment and perfection of form.[6] Although Le Corbusier did not affiliate himself with any religious tradition per se, his search for the ineffable became an inherent characteristic of his own design of sacred space. In this regard, the idea of the ineffable simultaneously alludes to that which *cannot* be said, because it is beyond words, and that which *should not* be said, because it is too holy for words.

Reinforcing Le Corbusier's vision of sacred space was the French journal *L'Art Sacré*, edited by the Dominican Marie-Alain Couturier (1897–1954). As a vehicle for the intellectual and artistic outpouring of thinking regarding mid-twentieth-century sacred art and design, the journal advocated for the intentional convergence of modern art, architecture, and spirituality. The Chapelle du Rosaire in Vence by Henri Matisse (1869–1954), part of a Dominican community just outside of Nice, was one of the most fully complete embodiments of this aspiration. Matisse designed all aspects of this total work of art—even including a colorful set of liturgical vestments—near the end of his life, during the years 1947–1951. His stated ambition was "to inscribe a spiritual space," which he realized through the careful deployment of panes of brilliantly colored glass (green, blue, and yellow) which surround a small interior space clad with white tiles. The three elements of simplicity of form, radiance of light, and vividness of color create the effect of the space being bathed in what one recent observer described as "waves of liquid, colored light."[7] The interior walls of the chapel are boldly inscribed with Matisse's large-scale, minimalist-brushstroke sketches of the Stations of the Cross, a Madonna and Child, and a figure of St. Dominic behind the altar. [Figure 1] At the time of the chapel's completion, Matisse himself declared it his masterpiece, and it was, of course, featured in a celebratory issue of *L'Art Sacré*.[8]

Figure 2

    The twentieth-century exploration of architectural innovation in sacred building also moved beyond the traditional borders of European/American Christianity. New sacred buildings inspired by International Modernism were widely disseminated around the globe in what might be termed a modernist diaspora. In Mexico, for example, Felix Candela (1910–1997) deployed a hyperbolic paraboloid shell of reinforced concrete for religious works during the 1950s and 1960s. Then, in 1971, French architects André-Jacques Dunoyer de Segonzac (1915–2018), Pierre Dupré (1913–2009), and Pierre Domino built the monumental Basílica Catedral Nuestra Señora de la Altagracia in Salvaleón de Higüey (Dominican Republic), based on concrete parabolic form. In recent decades, China has witnessed the construction of many new modern religious centers, chapels, and churches to meet the needs of its growing Christian population, on track to become the world's largest. One recent example is the Suzhou Chapel (2016) by the Shanghai architects Neri & Hu: a white cubical volume set atop an irregular brick platform. By way of historical example, these are but a small sampling of the extensive instances of how modern sacred architecture has been deployed and adapted in non-Western regions.

    The current of modern church design entered a particularly prolific period in the decades on either side of the 2000 millennium. The

Roman Catholic dioceses in and around Paris, for instance, undertook a building program to erect churches in neighborhoods not well served by traditional parishes. One such church is La Maison d'Église Notre Dame de Pentecôte (1998–2001), strategically located in the La Defense business district on the west side of the city. Designed by Franck Hammoutène (1954–2021), it is not a parish church per se, but intended as an outreach to those who work in the surrounding office towers—a place of "meeting, openness to all, and reconciliation between culture and faith." [Figure 2] The architect deemed it "a place of solitude and a place of communion, perfectly public and perfectly private," and the Bishop of the Diocese of Nanterre called it a "laboratory" for offering spiritual experience to a secularized, laicized society.[9]

The millennial building surge also resulted in a number of new cathedrals. In addition to Moneo's design for the Los Angeles Cathedral, other significant projects included the Cathedral of Christ the Light in Oakland, California (2008) by SOM's Craig Hartman; Mario Botta's Cathédral de la Résurrection (1995) in Evry, France; Sacred Heart Cathedral in Kericho, Kenya (2015) by the British firm John McAslan & Partners; and the Cathedral of the Northern Lights (2013) above the Arctic Circle in Alta, Norway by Schmidt Hammer Lassen Architects of Denmark.[10] In addition to these larger works, other celebratory buildings marking the turn of the millennium were also commissioned, such as Richard Meier's iconic Jubilee Church of Dio Padre Misericordioso, Rome (2003).

SINCE THE CREATION of such major projects as these, however, one notices in subsequent years a turn in much new sacred architecture toward more discrete projects that reflect a greater interiority of spirit, often with no overtly explicit religious affiliation. This turn is reflected in the Vatican's "Chapels Pavilion" at the 2018 Venice Biennale. Curated by Francesco Dal Co, the exhibition featured ten small chapels gathered in a wooded area, designed by ten different architects from around the world. The only requirement was that each chapel have an altar and a lectern, and many of them are abstract constructions intended as simple, private meditative spaces.[11] [Figure 3] On a similar note, one particularly interesting project is the Ruta del Peregrino (Pilgrim's Route, 2011), created by Mexico City architects Tatiana Bilbao and Derek Dellekamp, working with a team of young international architects. Built as a series of nine shelters, chapels, and

A remarkable outpouring of new sacred works has challenged the very idea of what a religious building is.

lookout points along the 117-kilometer pilgrimage route from the town of Ameca to the Marian church in Talpa de Allende (Jalisco), the project is as much land art as architecture, leaving individual pilgrims to experience and interpret the installations for themselves.[12]

Another recent turn in sacred architecture is toward a more conscious embrace of the needs of neighborhood communities, focusing on sacred buildings as sites of gathering and connection. In fact, a study by Partners for Sacred Places suggests that a neighborhood's economic vitality is tied in part to the strength of its faith communities. As Michael Crosbie has pointed out, one manifestation of this turn is the emphasis placed by so-called divergent churches "on life and what makes it meaningful" rather than on maintaining the church as a doctrinally and liturgically based institution.[13] He cites St. Lydia's Dinner Church in Brooklyn, where architect Sheryl Jordan transformed a storefront into a sacred space of welcome, hospitality, and intimacy.

A rather different example of a turn toward the neighborhood is Rafael Moneo's Iglesia de Iesu (2001–2009) in the newly developed Riberas de Loiola section of San Sebastián, Spain. Here, the architect eschews the temptation to erect a scenographic building calling attention to itself and chooses instead an "understated composition of white cubes" (even including a basement supermarket as a point of connection with the community).[14] The commission gave Moneo an opportunity to return to the challenge of sacred building after the Los Angeles Cathedral. Some critics have observed that the strength of the underlying design austerity of the Cathedral was "fatally compromised" by the insertion of works of literal religious symbolism (such as a series of enormous tapestries on each side of the nave depicting with figural-realism Christian saints in procession). By contrast, in San Sebastián, Moneo was given the freedom by the parish priest to provide the faithful "with a space that allowed them to express their religious feelings without any interference." As Moneo summarized his task, "The purer the form and the less conventional the iconography the better."[15] The result is a church whose pure white asceticism, bathed in natural light from rooftop lanterns, evokes the quintessential modernism of the St. Fronleichnam (Corpus Christi) Church in Aachen (1928–1939), built by the religious and architectural theorist Rudolf Schwarz (1897–1961). Interestingly, in a discussion of the Iesu Church, *The Architectural Review* explicitly identifies the new building as having achieved Le Corbusier's ideal of "the domain of the ineffable." [Figure 4] To echo Romano Guardini (1885–1968), the Italian theologian of liturgical renovation, one might say that it is not so much a void but that it exudes a tremendous quiet in which images have been voluntarily relinquished to favor instead an intense, individual spiritual perception.[16]

A culturally significant contribution made by modern sacred architecture is an overt embrace of regional cultural identities. Many recent examples of sacred building are inflected with a pronounced awareness of local specificity. This conscious understanding of the value of the local stands against any idea of a universal language of the sacred, upholding instead the importance of identity and place in the face of

Figure 3

Figure 4

the ubiquitous placelessness imposed by global capitalism. To mention by way of example one very recent project: In late 2022, the Italian firm Mixtura completed a monastic complex for the Convent of the Franciscan Fraternity of Bethany in one of the most volatile neighborhoods of Salvador de Bahia (Brazil) that draws heavily on the use of locally sourced native wood cladding, opening out to the temperate sea breezes of the coastal town. The complex is designed with a contextually attuned language that supports a mixed-use program open to the city's residents, even while providing the necessary reclusion for the conventual community.[17]

Any account of contemporary sacred architecture would be incomplete without acknowledging, even in passing, a redefinition and broadening of the genre of sacred work through an examination of the role monuments and memorials have as a means for communities and even nations to tell their stories. In recent decades especially, many communities have found suitable responses to painful, era-defining moments through architectural interventions. One thinks, for example, of the history of the lynching of African Americans in the United States, now remembered in the National Memorial for Peace and Justice, Montgomery, Alabama designed by MASS Design Group (2018); or the more remote seventeenth-century episode of burning witches in Vardø, Norway which is recollected through the Steilneset Memorial by Peter Zumthor (2011).

The examples of sacred architecture cited here barely scratch the surface of the immense productivity of architects who have taken the risk of attempting to design spiritually meaningful contemporary buildings. Writing in July 2020, at the height of the COVID-19 pandemic, architect Duo Dickinson observed that sacred architecture "connects us to what transcends our fears," with the power "to evoke the best in us."[18] Even this brief excursus shows that to attempt such a construction today stands apart as a provocative assertion of connective meaning. The distinctive narrative that sacred building has historically provided within modern architecture suggests that it can take a critical yet precarious stance that says more, even, than the architect may at first intend. •

Prayer and Struggle, Stephen Pavey, 2019, Dr. Wendsler Nosie, Sr. with granddaughter Báase Pike, San Carlos Apache Reservation, AZ. Used with permission.

Visual Storytelling and Walking with the Oppressed:

A Journey to Our Sacred Unity

By Stephen Pavey

ART AND SPIRITUALITY

111

Love is known when we recognize our self in the other. We are then no longer other, and that's the ecstasy of love.

—Richard Rohr

I FELL IN LOVE with photography as a child. I learned largely through practice how to master all the settings and manage variables to capture light. But it would be decades later, through facing my own darkness on the cusp of the second half of life, before I would discover another source of light I was not seeing. It was not light to be captured by a camera or a photo to be taken, but rather light to be experienced.

The healing light I was discovering as our sacred unity created a change in my relationship to the camera and to the world I was photographing. Now, rather than document or take photos from communities, photography has become a contemplative practice of visual storytelling with and alongside communities in our collective struggle for freedom. Creating art and telling stories with photographs is no longer for me about the production of a photograph as an end. Rather, creating art is a means of learning to see reality as it is and as it could be. Art has become like prayer, a way to pay attention.

Central to my practice of photography is accompanying and being accompanied by all who are marginalized and dehumanized by settler colonialism and capitalism. I accepted the invitation long ago from bell hooks (1952–2021) to come to the margins, where liberation is fomenting and where I am learning to see "the margins as more than a site of deprivation," but, rather, as "the site of radical possibility, a space of resistance . . . from which to see and create, to imagine alternatives, new worlds."[1] The camera now allows me to experience great suffering and great love at the margins of society, where our collective visual storytelling is used to organize, resist, and expose the lies of the dominant narrative of empire.

The photograph I've shared with this article, captioned "Prayer and Struggle," is of Dr. Wendsler Nosie, Sr. He is accompanied by his granddaughter Báásé Pike. It was taken at the moment he left behind the Nda (Apache) reservation, as he made his journey home to Chi'chil Bildagoteel (also known as Oak Flat), the mountains that are under threat of being destroyed by a multinational copper mining company, with support from the federal government.[2] I cannot think of a better photograph to share that captures the vocation I'm living as an artist engaged in contemplation and action in the world.

I first met Nosie, former chairman of the San Carlos Apache tribe and a spiritual leader of Apache-Stronghold, during a 2018 visit to Phoenix, where grassroots leaders were organizing efforts to join with the national Poor People's Campaign to confront the interlocking evils of systemic racism, poverty, ecological devastation, militarism and the war economy, and the distorted moral narrative of religious nationalism. Following that gathering, I made a trip with him back to Oak Flat to learn more about and to document the Apache struggle to protect this sacred land from an impending government transfer of it to the Resolution Copper project.

I thought I was there to learn more about their struggle as a single issue that could help inform how the Poor People's Campaign could better address the ecological devastation. However, I learned so much more. It was here that I first heard Nosie say, "In order to understand how to confront these interlocking evils, you must go back to the first chapter of how this country was founded." He was offering to help all of us go beyond our good intentions to make the world a better place and better understand how to confront these interlocking evils by decolonizing our analysis and organizing efforts. We need to go back to the first chapter to see how we can connect prayer and struggle so that we can journey toward our sacred unity and to the healing this world needs.

Apache-Stronghold has filed a lawsuit against the United States, and oral arguments have already been heard in the US Court of Appeals for the Ninth Circuit. Apache-Stronghold asked the court to protect the religious freedom of the Apache, which includes protecting the land at Oak Flat just as it would protect any church, mosque, or synagogue from government destruction. The Apache religion remains

> Art has become like prayer,
> a way to pay
> attention.

under threat as the government continues in its colonial history of failures to recognize the Apache's religious freedom, which cannot be separated from its way of life and the ceremony connected to Oak Flat and the earth. If the government gives Oak Flat to Resolution Copper, it will lead to the destruction of both that sacred land and the religion and identity of the Apache people.

While Oak Flat and the Apache spiritual way of life are under imminent threat, we also must open our eyes to see that all creation is under threat because of the greed of the US settler colonial and capitalist system that values profits and the interests of corporations over our responsibilities to each other and the earth.

Just before I created this photograph, Nosie had stopped at the boundary line of the San Carlos Apache reservation to lead a young Apache boy and myself to a private space near an aqueduct at the side of the road. He invited us to join him in a ceremony of healing and blessing. As he created a pool in the sand to collect the sacred rainwater, he spoke to us of his prayers for this journey. They were a way to let go of all his fears and hurt and to embrace who the Creator has made him to be. He said the lies and evil of the colonial system were designed to intentionally eradicate his true identity. As he poured the collected water over his head, he quietly declared, "I'm done being a victim, done negotiating with lies. I'm letting go of all the pain, all the hurt inflicted by the evil of this nation's way of life. I can now be Apache."

On this day, after sending a letter of notice to the US government,[3] Nosie left the reservation to establish permanent residence at Chi'chil Bildagoteel in order to protect the sacred Apache site, both for the religious freedom of the Apache and for all whose religious beliefs cannot be separated from their connection to Mother Earth. But Nosie was not only walking off the reservation, where his people have been held as prisoners and wards of the state. He was walking away from the colonizer's way of death to return to the spiritual way of life intended by the Creator.

After he finished with his prayer, Nosie invited us to join him in taking the same journey of healing to sacred unity by remembering who we were as humans and as relatives. I will never forget that day. It brings together all that I continue to experience at the intersection of visual storytelling, contemplation, and struggle.

Prayer and struggle are always connected.

It is at the margins of empire that I'm learning how spirituality is embodied in the world as love through contemplation and struggle with communities like Apache-Stronghold. Nosie and Apache-Stronghold teach us that it is the evils of capitalism and colonialism that have cut us all off from the one spirit that connects all beings. These systems have coopted our religions, Nosie tells us, disconnecting us from the one spirit and alienating us from ourselves, each other, and our Mother Earth. His call for all religions, including Christianity, to find their way back home echoes the words of the mystic Howard Thurman (1899–1981):

> Too often the price exacted by society for security and respectability is that the Christian movement in its formal expression must be on the side of the strong against the weak. This is a matter of tremendous significance, for it reveals to what extent a religion that was born of a people acquainted with persecution and suffering has become the cornerstone of a civilization and of nations whose very position in modern life too often has been secured by a ruthless use of power applied to weak and defenseless peoples.[4]

The lies of capitalism tell us that we are what we own, what we produce, what we sell, what we extract, and what we dominate. But through prayer from any tradition, Nosie tells us we can begin to heal by remembering who we are. From here, we can begin to live into our sacred unity, and when we are able to remember who we are and reconnect to all that is sacred, we will then be challenged to enter into resistance and struggle against all that desecrates and destroys. Prayer and struggle are always connected.

The spiritual path for me toward sacred unity can never only be about a personal experience of love that ignores our collective struggle for liberation. I see love and liberation being forged between resistance and struggle and contemplative prayer. Cocreating visual stories through photography with communities on the margins is helping me to see and embody love and liberation in the world. Thomas Merton (1915–1968), in the last year of his life, spoke of the mystics that will help guide us. Wendsler Nosie, Sr. is one of those mystics and prophets that Merton wrote about, conveying the same message that the Apache and many indigenous communities share, if only we had eyes to see and ears to hear:

> I stand among you as one who offers a small message of hope, that first, there are always people who dare to seek on the margin of society, who are not dependent on social acceptance, not dependent on social routine, and prefer a kind of free-floating existence under a state of risk. And among these people, if they are faithful to their own calling, to their own vocation, and to their own message from God, communication on the deepest level is possible. And the deepest level of communication is not communication, but communion. It is wordless. It is beyond words, and it is beyond speech and beyond concept. Not that we discover a new unity. We discover an older unity. My dear brothers [and sisters], we are already one. But we imagine that we are not. And what we have to recover is our original unity. What we have to be is what we are.[5] •

As I Sit Thinking in the Car

I love her. And I fail her. And I love that
my failing does not put an end to Love.
Which says more about her than it does me.
More about Love than it does me. More about
how we are all more than one thing. All earth,
rocking and reeling and spilling over with glory.
Grand Canyons, the sum of us, cracked and
carrying the brushstrokes of God.
Each a natural wonder.

—Drew Jackson[1]

RECOMMENDED READING

Art + Faith: A Theology of Making
Makoto Fujimura
Yale University Press, 2020

A Book Review by Lee Staman

MAKOTO FUJIMURA WAS BORN IN Boston but spent his childhood in Japan before returning to the United States. His painting style is part of what some call the "slow art" movement. Fujimura specializes in the Japanese technique called *nihonga*. This particular style emphasizes organic materials and often uses precious metals. In Fujimura's case, he will often use gold, among other metals, to create massive abstract-expressionist paintings that have struck me as glimpses of something wild and untamed.

In *Art + Faith: A Theology of Making*, Fujimura describes the process involved with making art in the style of *nihonga*. His description is beautiful and immersive, much like his paintings. The process of *nihonga* is almost painstakingly slow, as the materials are ground into fine particles before use. To commemorate the four-hundred-year anniversary of the King James Bible, he was commissioned to illuminate a new manuscript consisting of five major frontispieces, eighty-nine chapter-heading letters, and 148 illumined pages. The painting he did for the Gospel of Mark, called "Water Flames," is a swirling orange-and-red conflagration that looks at once both warming and consuming. Many of Fujimura's massive canvases require patience in the making and patience in the appreciating. They resist speedy consumption and instead envelop the viewer with depth, color, and movement.

In *Art + Faith*, Fujimura follows a similar train of thought that he explored in *Culture Care*, namely that for us to move forward, our lives must be slow and purposeful with an emphasis on generative "making." The book itself is an exploration of what it means to be an artist and, in Fujimura's case, a Christian artist. He does a good job of being honest about how Christianity—more specifically, conservative Protestant Christianity—has been wary of artistic endeavors. He writes, "Imagination, like art, has often been seen as suspect by some Christians who perceive the art world as an assault upon traditional values. These expectations of art are largely driven by fear that art will lead us away from 'truth' into an anarchic freedom of expression."[1]

He goes on to state that in his experience, explaining art is often easier with non-Christians because the Christians he encounters tend to have a more analytical approach (to determine whether something is true or not), a more factually based approach to faith and spirituality. In the book, he calls this sort of approach to God and the spiritual life "plumbing theology." Such theology is focused on utilitarian answers and ways of being in the world. Fujimura is critical of faith and life being driven by what is "useful." He writes, "The path of creativity gives wings. The essential question is not whether we are religious, but whether we are making something. When we stop making, we become enslaved to market culture as mere consumers."[2]

Connected to this was a part of the book I very much enjoyed, namely, his chapter on the Japanese art of *kintsugi*, where lacquer is mixed with powdered gold to fix broken pieces of pottery. This practice is rich with metaphor and meaning in Buddhism, where it is linked to the Japanese aesthetic of *wabi-sabi*, which appreciates the transience, impermanence, and beauty that is found in simplicity. Fujimura draws out a Christian meaning from this artform as well. As Fujimura sees it, this reimagined brokenness is indicative of our New Creation in Christ. His take on *kintsugi* is also a reminder that broken pottery mended with precious metals is an antithesis to consumerism and mass production. It is a physical reminder of the power of sustainability.

While I enjoyed much of this book, there were moments when his Reformed or neo-Reformed American Protestant Christianity came out in rather odd ways that did not seem congruent with the book as a whole. I got the sense that he needed to place these sorts of Calvinistic hallmarks in the book (e.g., our utter worthlessness in the face of

God's overwhelming goodness and power and the idea of substitutionary atonement) because this is the sort of Christianity with which he is familiar. Unfortunately, these snippets of Reformed theology appeared as sharp breaks within the broader "theology of making" that he is trying to convey. I think a book like Belden C. Lane's *Ravished by Beauty: The Surprising Legacy of Reformed Spirituality* would provide a better grasp on traditional Reformed theology.

In the end, *Art + Faith: A Theology of Making* perhaps works best as a starting point rather than a systematic treatment, which is more than sufficient for a theology that stresses generative making. Much like his art, Fujimura's writing is layered, inviting readers into a profound conversation. But, unlike art, writing does require a little more direction, and *Art + Faith* does meander at times without claiming a clear purpose.

When Fujimura engages in theology and art, there are many moments where there is not enough thoughtful consideration or depth of discussion of either. He makes statements like, "Theology, too, must be thought of as an organic layer of growth, rather than as a mechanistic, rational argument only. Theology must grow and be sown into the soils of culture, be fed by spring rains of love to be cultivated into multiple generations,"[3] but then he does not explore where this beautiful thought might go. This leaves the reader wanting more of either one or the other.

In my opinion, Fujimura is more in his element when discussing art and the process of art than he is in the realm of theological contemplation. More on *nihonga* and *kintsugi* would have spoken volumes. Overall, he advocates something I wholeheartedly agree with: a necessary slowing down and a patience. Toward the end of the book, he captures this sentiment beautifully when he writes:

> The art of waiting depends upon our willingness to die to ourselves and trust in God. Art, poetry, and music all depend on waiting. There is no music without pauses. There is no art if we are unwilling to wait for paint to dry. More significantly, the process of making mimics what we need to learn to do in life. Holy Saturday is the critical day on which we are invited to die to ourselves. When we are able to fully die to ourselves, we will hear the voice of God on Easter morning.[4] •

RECOMMENDED VIEWING

American Symphony

Directed by Matthew Heineman
Netflix, 2023

A Film Review by Paul Swanson

> *Art can amplify the sacred and challenge the status quo.*
> —Dr. Barbara Holmes[1]

> *We play music to communicate unspoken pain and joy.*
> —Jon Batiste[2]

VIRTUES LURE ME INTO SITTING in the front pew before the pulpit of music. As a devotee in the service of love, music is my preferred preacher. The family stereo of my 1980s childhood home spun a particular set of records: Neil Diamond, Fats Domino, and Bob Dylan. This early education cultivated the conditions for me to attune to the ineffable qualities of music. Feeling the gentle knocking of knuckles on my heart, I learned to listen for specific brandished fruits—faith, joy, humility, and truth.

Earworms come and go, but songs that exude these virtues are sung out of eternity. They hit a deathless frequency at ease with shattering pop charts or being hushed in dank basement clubs. Songs of healing and flourishing help me breathe more deeply and freely before the grimacing face of reality. I was reminded of this while watching *American Symphony*, a documentary that follows multi-hyphenate musician Jon Batiste on the joys, resistances, and travails of embodying this sacred soul task: creating music of flourishing and healing. When the end credits rolled and my ears were treated to another song by Batiste, I could feel knuckles tapping at my heart. Jon Batiste creates a noetic and virtuous atmosphere that breathes freely.

When words are necessarily limited, focus tightens. This review of *American Symphony* will narrow in on Jon Batiste as a public contemplative of the arts.[3]

THE GROUND OF LOVE

In *American Symphony*, viewers witness the artistic path of Jon Batiste at the height of his public powers—as *The Late Show* bandleader, Grammy-nominated artist, and Carnegie Hall bound. And then we learn the grim news that leukemia has returned to Suleika Jaouad, his wife. Rather than unseat the creative journey as the center of the film, this news sadly brightens the headline that was already printed in their relationship. Love is the beginning, end, and way of artistry in their lives. Creativity is the outpouring of their love: A tear-stained, scarred love that has learned to shred expectations on arrival. A love that dances on. *American Symphony* lives and breathes as a celebratory exhibition of creativity as the way of love.

PRESSURE, PARADOX, AND THE PAUSE

The documentary's title, *American Symphony*, shares its name with the symphony that Jon Batiste is writing to premiere at Carnegie Hall. The symphony serves as the brooding architectural backdrop for the entire film. Cradling the responsibilities of work, vision, and family, Batiste realizes something has to give. He says, "I am trying to expand the canon of symphonic music, break through long gate-kept spaces, and all without having the space in my life carved out to focus on it."[4] Batiste's ambition is to draw out a transcendent symphony already suspended in the air of America, to gather all facets of American music genres, traditions, and cultures into one symphonic exhalation that *we the people* can breathe together. And to give himself the breathing space to create, Batiste decreases his constraints. He steps away from a spotlight holding him back from expanding his vision and tending to his family. He leaves his post as bandleader of *The Late Show*.

It takes humility to see that among an array of dream-come-true opportunities there is a blockade to fulfilling a vision. Herein lies the mettle of Batiste's artistic vision. Even when wise discernment among competing priorities leads to a clearing away of what stands in the way, it both relieves external pressure and can tighten internal ones. Having experienced panic attacks and anxiety in the past, Batiste knows an inward weight is still required to see his vision through. He names the mounting pressure he feels as a Black artist, his worry over Jaouad's health, and the anxiety over the stakes of his creative potential. This pressure is ultimately not relieved, but a paradox to be breathed into.

Jon Batiste humbly holds the paradoxes of life. We observe this in the profound way gratitude is always acknowledged within mind-numbing pressure. In response to the question of whether or not it is important for him to exude positivity, he thoughtfully pauses and then says,

> I'm grateful to be here. I'm grateful to have these words memorialized, and, whatever that is gonna do in the world, I believe that has a serious impact, and I want that impact to lead to joy. I want that impact to lead to someone being uplifted or healed. That's a real thing. That's very real. But they also have Black people cooning and mugging for the camera and smiling and dancing for centuries, and that was all that people could see them as. So, we really have a psychosis in terms of how we perceive Black entertainers and Black intellectuals. We have something to actually overcome to understand the full range of what they offer to the world. And sometimes we don't see that until after the fact. So, it's important that I also state that too.[5]

In a question that could be batted away as flattery or leading, Batiste holds up the paradox. He walks the pressure into the paradox of quietude and charisma, celebration and sorrow, faith and fortune, and, of course, life and death. And he invites the listener to join him in the paradox, a responsibility needed to honor songs of flourishing and healing.

Paradoxical breathing room provides Jon Batiste the audacity of the pause. This is why Batiste is a public contemplative of the arts.

Throughout the film, when overwhelm casts a shadow overhead, he pauses. We witness him in prayer and meditation. We see him go to the quiet touch of his beloved. We see him go to nature or turn to music. We see him reach out to his friends or a therapist. We bear the physical silence that appears to protect and nourish him.

There is a distinctive moment midway through the film that hallows his pause. Sitting on stage before a crowded concert hall, Batiste dedicates a song to Jaouad, still awaiting her bone-marrow transplant. And then he pauses. He leans heavy on the pause, *for over a minute*. Seemingly doing nothing, Batiste holds a reverent posture with eyelids closed and hands hovering over the keys. We can feel him amassing the power of presence. And when he finally plays, it flutters between passionate restraint and unbridled cries of the heart.

This was as ardent and freeing a contemplative act as his foot-stomping, get-out-of-your-chair-and-dance performance at the Grammys. It dawned on me then that these two seemingly divergent acts were born from the same pause. Jon Batiste walks in paradoxes, creates out of the pause, and then breathes life into that creation. Dancing yet standing still. This is what creating out of the pause looks like.

There is a soundscape I want to pass on and instruct my kids with, to edify and exemplify the ineffable power of song. At the center is music that enjoys inspirited fruits. Jon Batiste is an artist that I play on repeat in hopes that my family catches the cogent and contagious contemplative spirit that pours through each pause and breath of his artistry. *American Symphony* embodies the radicality of Batiste's creative genius as a contemplative vessel in service to freedom and love amidst all the suffering and pressure, resulting in songs of flourishing and healing. That is the American Symphony I want my kids to be raised in. ◆

NOTES

Introduction
1 See Contemplify, https://contemplify.com/pod/.
2 Richard Rohr, *Dancing Standing Still: Healing the World from a Place of Prayer* (Mahwah, NJ: Paulist, 2014), 1.

Accordion
1 Teddy Macker, "Accordion," © 2022, previously unpublished.

The Artist's Access to Mystery
1 *The Ascension of Christ* by Hans Süss von Kulmbach is currently installed at the Metropolitan Museum of Art in New York City.
2 Adapted from Richard Rohr, *The Universal Christ: How a Forgotten Reality Can Change Everything We See, Hope For, and Believe* (New York: Convergent, 2018), 118–119.

The Art of Food
1 Kongdej Jaturanrasamee, *Hunger* (Bangkok: Netflix, 2023).

Joshua: 45-46
1 Josh Radnor, "Joshua: 45-46," *Eulogy: Volume 1*, November 17, 2023, https://www.joshradnor.com/jr-store/p/eulogy-volume-i-vinyl.

Discovering My Soul
1 "The Gender Gap in Religion Around the World," *Pew Research Center*, March 22, 2016, https://www.pewresearch.org/religion/2016/03/22/the-gender-gap-in-religion-around-the-world/.

With New Eyes

1. Marcel Proust, *The Prisoner*, trans. Carol Clark (New York: Penguin Classics, 2019).

When Body Speaks: On Dance as Spiritual Practice

1. A conscious dance modality developed by dancer and musician Gabrielle Roth (1941–2021).
2. As Dr. Barbara Holmes writes, bodily prayer is "the beginning of pilgrimage from ordinary to sacred space." Barbara Holmes, *Joy Unspeakable: Contemplative Practices of the Black Church*, 2nd ed. (Minneapolis: Fortress, 2017), 77.
3. Bonnie Badenoch, *The Heart of Trauma: Healing the Embodied Brain in the Context of Relationships* (New York: W.W. Norton, 2017), 41.
4. Badenoch, *The Heart of Trauma*, 46.
5. See the concept of the "soul nerve" in Resmaa Menakem, *My Grandmother's Hands: Racialized Trauma and the Pathway to Mending Our Hearts and Bodies* (Las Vegas: Central Recovery Press, 2017), 4.
6. We become "more comfortable listening to the language of sensation side by side with the more familiar world of words. . . . As we attend, our bodies seem to share more information." Badenoch, *The Heart of Trauma*, 134.
7. Menakem, *My Grandmother's Hands*, 19.
8. "Somatic therapies can help patients to relocate themselves in the present by experiencing that it is safe to move. Feeling the pleasure of taking effective action restores a sense of agency and a sense of being able to actively defend and protect themselves." Bessel A. van der Kolk, *The Body Keeps the Score: Brain, Mind, and Body in the Healing of Trauma* (New York: Penguin, 2015), 321.
9. "We encode 11 million bits of sensory information per second perceptually (implicitly) while encoding six to fifty bits consciously (explicitly)." Badenoch, *The Heart of Trauma*, xii.
10. van der Kolk, *The Body Keeps the Score*, 151.
11. van der Kolk, *The Body Keeps the Score*, 485.
12. "Kofi Agawu says that 'rhythm refers to a binding together of different dimensional processes, a joining rather than a separating, an across-the-dimensions instead of within-the-dimension phenomenon.' At the very least, there is an embodied knowing that exceeds the limits of rational thought." Dr. Barbara Holmes, *Joy Unspeakable*, 41.

Meeting a Creative God in the Arts

1. See Matthew Fox, *Prayer: A Radical Response to Life* (New York: Tarcher/Putnam, 2001).
2. Adam Frank, *The Constant Fire: Beyond the Science vs. Religion Debate* (Berkeley, CA: University of California Press, 2009), 152.
3. See Margaret Mann Phillips, *Erasmus and the Northern Renaissance* (New York: Macmillan, 1950), 212.
4. Karl Barth, as quoted in John de Gruchy, *Christianity, Art and Transformation: Theological Aesthetics in the Struggle for Justice* (Cambridge, UK: Cambridge University Press, 2001), 122.

The Abbey as Art Repository

1. Felix Lopez, "Creation of Our Lady of Guadalupe Bulto for Santa Maria de la Vid Abbey," undated flyer.

The Persistent Resurgence of Sacred Architecture

1. Mario Botta, "Sacred Space," in *Architetture del Sacro: Prayers in Stone* (Bologna: Editrice Compositori, 2005), 12.
2. "Álvaro Siza and Alexandros N. Tombazis in Conversation," *Arquitectura ibérica*, special edition on Holy Trinity Church, Fátima, September 2007, 92.
3. See, for example, *Architectural Digest*'s list of "The 12 Most Spectacular Modern Churches," compiled by Elizabeth Stamp, August 17, 2023, https://www.architecturaldigest.com/gallery/worlds-most-spectacular-modern-churches; or *Arch2o*'s "25 Visionary Modernist Churches: Embracing Innovation in Worship," https://www.arch2o.com/25-visionary-modern-churches-embracing-innovation-in-worship/.
4. Jürgen Habermas, "The Resurgence of Religion: A Challenge to the Secular Self-Understanding of Modernity," The Castle Lectures, Yale University, October 2008.
5. Rafael Moneo, "Architecture as a Vehicle for Religious Experience: The Los Angeles Cathedral," in Karla Cavarra Britton, ed., *Constructing the Ineffable* (New Haven: Yale University Press, 2010), 159.
6. Le Corbusier, "L'Espace indicible," *L'Architecture d'Aujourd'hui*, January 1946, 9–10.
7. Sebastian Smee, "I've seen plenty of beautiful artworks. But the Matisse Chapel overwhelmed me," *Washington Post*, August 8, 2019,

https://www.washingtonpost.com/entertainment/museums/ive-seen-plenty-of-beautiful-artworks-but-the-matisse-chapel-overwhelmed-me/2019/08/07/4734f070-b550-11e9-951e-de024209545d_story.html.

8 M. A. Couturier, L. B. Rayssiguier, and J. de Laprade, "Vence," introduction by Henri Matisse, *L'Art sacré* 11–12, July/August 1951.

9 *La Maison d'Église Notre Dame de Pentecôte*, https://ndp92.fr.

10 Eric Baldwin, "Sacred Light: New Cathedral Rethinking Modern Worship," *ArchDaily*, January 20, 2022, https://www.archdaily.com/975440/sacred-light-new-cathedrals-rethinking-modern-worship.

11 Ellie Stathaki, "Cutting-edge Religious Architecture Around the World, *Wallpaper**, October 6, 2022, https://www.wallpaper.com/gallery/architecture/cutting-edge-religious-architecture-around-the-world.

12 "Mexico's Architectural Project: Ruta del Perigrino," *Icon: Architecture*, April 8, 2011, https://www.iconeye.com/architecture/mexico-s-architectural-project, ruta-del-peregrino.

13 Cited in Michael J. Crosbie, "Sacred Architecture Isn't Disappearing–It's Changing," *Common/Edge*, December 26, 2019, https://commonedge.org/sacred-architecture-isnt-disappearing-its-changing/.

14 Michael Webb, "Rafael Moneo's Iesu Church in San Sebastian, Spain," *Architectural Review*, May 1, 2012, https://www.architectural-review.com/today/rafael-moneos-iesu-church-in-san-sebastian-spain.

15 Rafael Moneo, "Architecture as a Vehicle for Religious Experience: The Los Angeles Cathedral" in *Constructing the Ineffable: Contemporary Sacred Architecture*, ed. Karla Cavarra Britton (New Haven, CT: Yale School of Architecture, 2010).

16 "Corpus Christi Church, Aachen," *Arquitectura Viva*, https://arquitecturaviva.com/works/iglesia-del-corpus-aquisgran.

17 Stefan Novokovic, "In Brazil a Convent that Embraces Community," *Azure*, June 14, 2023, https://www.azuremagazine.com/article/salvador-de-bahia-convent-mixtura-architects-brazil/.

18 Duo Dickinson, "What Is Sacred Space?" *ArchDaily*, July 4, 2020, https://www.archdaily.com/942712/what-is-sacred-space.

Visual Storytelling and Walking with the Oppressed: A Journey to Our Sacred Unity

1 bell hooks, "Choosing the Margin as a Space of Radical Openness," *Yearning: Race, Gender, and Cultural Politics* (Boston: South End, 1990), 145–153.

2 To learn more about Apache-Stronghold and the struggle to protect Apache religion and Chi'chil Bildagoteel, see their website, www.apache-stronghold.com.

3 See Nosie's letter to the US government here: http://users.neo.registeredsite.com/8/3/2/11897238/assets/Nosie_Letter_to_FS_November_21_updated.pdf.

4 Howard Thurman, *Jesus and the Disinherited* (Boston: Beacon, 1976), 11–12.

5 Thomas Merton, *The Asian Journal of Thomas Merton* (New York: New Directions, 1975), 307–308.

As I Sit Thinking in the Car

1 Drew Jackson, "As I Sit Thinking in the Car," © 2022, previously unpublished.

Recommended Reading

1 Makoto Fujimura, *Art and Faith: A Theology of Making* (New Haven: Yale University Press, 2020), 5.

2 Fujimura, *Art and Faith*, 24.

3 Fujimura, *Art and Faith*, 72.

4 Fujimura, *Art and Faith*, 134.

Recommended Viewing

1 Barbara Holmes, *Joy Unspeakable: Contemplative Practices of the Black Church* (Minneapolis, MN: Fortress, 2017), 184.

2 Matthew Heineman, *American Symphony* (Netflix, 2023), documentary.

3 This film, like a cake, is layered with meaning. Seeing the impossibility of sharing its depth as a whole, I dove my fork into one particular layer so you could sample its sweetness.

4 Heineman, *American Symphony*.

5 Heineman, *American Symphony*.

Acknowledgments

In passing the torch after more than a decade as Editor of this fine publication, I want to thank the following people who have been instrumental in making *Oneing* the exceptional, globally recognized journal it is today:

- Richard Rohr for his invaluable support and contributions to the publication these past many years;

- many extraordinary Advisory Board members, including David Benner, James Danaher, Ilia Delio, Sheryl Fullerton, Stephen Gaertner, and Ruth Patterson;

- my stellar Associate Editor Shirin McArthur for her keen editorial eye and insights;

- Nelson Kane, whose work on another publication inspired me to invite him to design the elegant simplicity of *Oneing*;

- the many contributors who have made this publication the exceptional journal it is today; and,

- last but not least, *Oneing*'s readership for your ongoing support and appreciation of the journal.

—Vanessa Guerin

Center for
Action and
Contemplation

A collision of opposites forms the cross of Christ.
One leads downward preferring the truth of the humble.
The other moves leftward against the grain.
But all are wrapped safely inside a hidden harmony:
One world, God's cosmos, a benevolent universe.